D1234066

Advance pra.

"The Fathers of the Church have so much to say and Mike Aquilina helps us clearly hear their voice. This book opens the reader to the wisdom of the Church's great living tradition. Here we find the Church Fathers' insights on some of the most important questions of our day: marriage, the defense of human life, and the meaning of human sexuality. A welcome guide for learning how to think with the mind of the Church."

—Most Reverend Donald W. Wuerl, Archbishop of Washington

"Mike Aquilina's ardent faith in Jesus and his informed love for the Church and for her traditions shine forth splendidly in *Roots of the Faith*. He manifests this love by presenting the teachings of the early Fathers of the Church on subjects of contemporary importance, such as the Mass, Confession, the Bible, marriage and family life, and the dignity of human life. Clear, lively, and imaginative, this is an excellent book for laity and clergy alike. It's not only informative, it's also fun to read."

—Fr. Thomas G. Weinandy, O.F.M, Cap., Executive Director for the Secretariat for Doctrine, United States Conference of Catholic Bishops

"It's a question every Christian has to ask—do I believe what the early Christians believed? Mike Aquilina looks at our Catholic faith and the faith of our fathers (and mothers) to give a clear answer—if you could hop in a time machine and go back to the Church in its infancy, you'd find the faith you know today. With a scholar's depth and a journalist's gift to make his subject engaging, Aquilina gives us a book to read with pen in hand in order to mark the good stuff that appears on every page."

—Robert Lockwood, author, *A Guy's Guide to the Good Life*

ROOTS OF THE FAITH

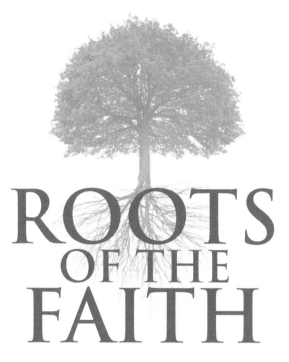

ROOTS
OF THE
FAITH

FROM THE CHURCH
FATHERS TO YOU

MIKE AQUILINA

SERVANT
BOOKS

PUBLISHED BY ST. ANTHONY MESSENGER PRESS
CINCINNATI, OHIO

Cover and book design by Mark Sullivan
Cover image © istockphoto.com | Dan Tero

LIBRARY OF CONGRESS CATALOGING-IN-PUBLICATION DATA
Aquilina, Mike.
Roots of the faith : from the church fathers to you / Mike Aquilina.
p. cm.
Includes bibliographical references (p.   ) and index.
ISBN 978-0-86716-938-6 (pbk. : alk. paper) 1. Catholic Church—Doctrines—
History. I. Title.
BX1747.A76 2010
230'.2—dc22

2010018468

ISBN 978-0-86716-938-6

Published by Servant Books, an imprint of St. Anthony Messenger Press.
28 W. Liberty St.
Cincinnati, OH 45202
www.AmericanCatholic.org
www.ServantBooks.org

Printed in the United States of America.

Printed on acid-free paper.

10 11 12 13 14   5 4 3 2 1

For Jack Nelson

CONTENTS

ACKNOWLEDGMENTS

"Every good endowment and every perfect gift is from above, coming down from the Father of lights" (James 1:17). If there is any good in this book, chalk it up to grace, and may it be to God's glory. His grace usually comes to me, however, through channels.

I am grateful to our ancestors in the faith, for the lives they lived, for the Sacred Tradition they kept faithfully and passed on to us, and for the other records and relics they left behind, sometimes quite by accident: beautiful literature, of course, but also great works of art, churches that have stood for centuries, pious graffiti scrawled on ancient walls, and homey devotions worked into the fabric of household items, from oil lamps to window sashes.

I am particularly grateful to the Church Fathers whose writings are the framework of this book. There are several English editions of their documents. For this book I always began with three of the great collections produced in the nineteenth century: *The Ante-Nicene Fathers*, *The Nicene and Post-Nicene Fathers* (two series), and *The Apostolic Fathers*. The first two collections emerged from the University of Edinburgh in Scotland. The third was translated and annotated by the Anglican bishop J.B. Lightfoot. The English language has undergone major changes since these were published. So I have taken the liberty of updating the translations after consulting other translations and, whenever possible, the texts in the original languages. I'm grateful, as always, for the help of Chris Bailey, my brilliant and multilingual friend and colleague.

Good ideas come from Cindy Cavnar of Servant Books. Once on paper, they're cleaned up by editor Lucy Scholand.

But the writing's made possible by my wife of twenty-five years, Terri. She's my encouragement, my inspiration, my motivation—and she makes me laugh. St. John Chrysostom reportedly spoke of woman as "delectable mischief" (see chapter nine). I can't prove it, but I'm pretty sure he was prophesying about someone I know.

Witnesses to Tradition

A tiny baby grows into a child, an adolescent, a young adult, a parent. An acorn sprouts into a little seedling, then grows to a sapling, and finally to a great shady oak.

We watch the child grow and marvel to remember that there was once a newborn infant where now there is a responsible adult. We wonder how a mighty oak could ever rise from a tiny acorn. Yet the adult is still the same person as the child, and the tree is still the same plant.

Living things grow that way. The tree changes considerably as it grows and matures. In hindsight you can see in its early stages all the things you recognize in its maturity. Some are rudimentary and undeveloped, but they're still recognizable. The tree may have thousands of leaves where once it had two, but it hasn't become a different kind of tree.

The Catholic Church is a living organism, the body of Christ. It grew from a handful of mostly Jewish believers to the biggest religious body on earth, with more than a billion members worldwide. When we look back we can recognize in its very earliest stages all the things that make the Catholic Church distinct today. All the beliefs, all the sacraments, all the important practices of our Church today, go right back to the beginning. Nothing essential has been added, and nothing essential has been lost. We can see how things developed from twigs to branches, how one generation after another added its wisdom and its practice to the ever-growing tradition of the Church.

That's what this book is about. We're surrounded by a great cloud of witnesses, saints who went before us and left us snapshots of the Church they knew. We page through this family album and see our Church when it was taking its first steps, when it was growing into a strong youth, when it was maturing into a worldwide community. And through all those changes, we recognize the same Church.

That's not to say the changes were unimportant. Some of them have been very important.

Jesus Christ left us all we needed for the Christian religion. He spent three years training his disciples to be apostles, and they in turn spent many years training their successors. They passed down what they knew of the teachings of Christ—and just as importantly, what they remembered of the example he set in his life.

But we, imperfect humans that we are, only gradually come to understand what Christ taught us two millennia ago. Each generation works hard at understanding the teachings and the life of Christ and passes on what it has learned to the next generation. Guided by the Holy Spirit, the Church keeps the doctrines of Christ alive and slowly works toward a perfect understanding of them. That's what Tradition is. We will not have a perfect understanding until we reach heaven, but that's the goal we aim for.

Today, when historical revisionists would love to make us believe that the whole Catholic Church was an invention of the Middle Ages, our link with history is vital. We need to know that the Church is who she says she is—the divinely instituted body of

Christ whose Tradition goes right back to the apostles.

The truth is there for anyone to see. The evidence is clear. Our Catholic Church is the same Church Christ founded.

The Authority of the Ancients

The Church reserves a special reverence for the teachings of the Fathers. Who are these men?

The Church Fathers are the great teachers from the formative years, roughly the first seven centuries, of Christianity. They are the saints and thinkers who influenced the doctrine of the earliest councils, producing the creeds professed by Christians in every age. The Fathers are the monks and bishops who presided over the Church's worship—baptism, anointing, Eucharist—as the world's varied cultures produced the great liturgical families. The Fathers are the Spirit-led organizational geniuses who discerned the application of Church order—hierarchy and discipline—as Christianity spread far beyond Jerusalem. It was the Fathers who, by their fearless proclamation over the course of centuries, declared for the Church the canon of the Scriptures.

Most Christians, even non-Catholics, will acknowledge that the Fathers' teachings carry a certain weight. The *Catechism of the Catholic Church* tells us that the Fathers are "always timely witnesses" to the Church's tradition (*CCC*, 688). When we read the works of the Fathers, when we study the monuments they left behind, we can see the clear continuity from the ancient Church, the Church of the apostles and martyrs, to the Church in our own towns today, our own parishes.

Some decades ago a theologian named Joseph Ratzinger probed a little further and asked, more specifically, "What is the authority of the Church fathers?"[1] He answered that the Fathers are a constitutive and essential part of divine revelation.

God revealed himself definitively in Jesus Christ. He gave himself completely to the world through the incarnation of the Eternal Word. There was nothing more to say. Revelation, however, is like any communication. It involves a speaking and a listening—a giving and a receiving, a word and an *Amen*.

The words and lives of the Fathers mark the Church's great *Amen* to God's revelation. The Church sealed its acceptance, its commitment, its covenant, with the words of the councils and the blood of the martyrs. These flowed from a loving communion with the words and the blood of Jesus Christ. The great Amen of the Church resounds today in the unchanging canon of Scripture, in the forms of the liturgy, in the unshakeable structure of the Church, and in the godly morals by which Christians struggle to live in many diverse and hostile environments.

As we sing in the old hymn, the "Faith of our Fathers" is "living still, in spite of dungeon, fire, and sword." It lives on also in spite of the sins and infidelities of many who failed to live up to the patrimony our Fathers left for us. To this faith we pledge: "We will be true to thee till death."

Time Travel

In the pages of this book, I try to sketch out just a few matters related to the faith of the early Christians. The handful of issues I cover does not represent the key concerns of the Church Fathers. You'll find no chapters (for example) on the Trinity or on the natures and person of Jesus Christ. I steered clear of such essential matters because it would require the whole of the book to convey even a rough outline of the history of their discussion. Even the few topics I've chosen I'm able to treat only briefly in a book so small.

I chose to cover a handful of issues that interest me—issues I hope will interest you as well. I chose them because they are still contemporary—or once again contemporary.

In my telling of the story, I've drawn mostly from believers whose witness dates to the centuries of Roman persecution and the generations immediately afterward: the time of the formative councils of Nicaea, Constantinople, Ephesus, and Chalcedon. I refer not only to their writings but also, sometimes, to the works of their pagan adversaries. I draw occasional insights from archeology, epigraphy (the study of inscriptions and graffiti), and other sciences that shed light on those distant times.

And those times are distant only if we count by days. Counting by communion, they are as near as our parish church. For the faith of our Fathers is living still, and our Fathers are living still, as saints in heaven. They are that great cloud of witnesses; they are martyrs who cry out for us from heaven's altar (see Hebrews 12:1; Revelation 6:9–10).

We are, as I hope these chapters show, still living in the time of the early Christians. This world may spin on for four or forty or four hundred more millennia; and to our own distant descendants we will surely seem remote in our dress and customs. Yet those future generations should recognize their faith and life in the record we leave of our own faith and life; and our record should reflect, corroborate, and illumine the witness of the earliest Fathers.

So in the pages of this book—and, I hope, in our imagination and prayer—we turn to the witness and world of the Fathers. Theirs is a landscape that will seem strangely familiar. In fact, sometimes it'll seem almost like home.

CHAPTER ONE

The Mass: The Universal Sign

St. Peter's Basilica is the most colossal Catholic building on earth, holding up to sixty thousand people. A Mass there is a spectacle for all the senses: The art treasures of the ages look down on the celebration, glorious music fills the nave, the smell of incense drifts through the assembly, and colorful vestments light up the celebrants.

The scene is repeated on a smaller scale across the world. On every continent Masses are celebrated every day, in great cathedrals and tiny chapels, to congregations of thousands or where two or three are gathered in Jesus' name. The celebrations come in every language. The music may be the serenity of a plainsong chant, the majestic polyphony of Palestrina, or the well-worn hymns from our parish's well-worn hymnals.

But wherever we are, the basic parts of the Mass are the same. The same Mass can be dressed up in thousands of different vestments. And that simple observation tells us something profoundly important about the Mass.

The many local colors of the Mass show that traditions have been diverging for a long time. Christian populations, some of which have existed for centuries in near isolation from the rest of the

Church, have developed their own distinctive traditions around the Mass. But the differences are superficial: The fundamental identity of the Mass is the same everywhere.

And that tells us that the Mass must go back to the very earliest days of Christianity. Indeed, Luke tells us that after the Holy Spirit descended upon the apostles at Pentecost, "those who received [Peter's] word were baptized, and there were added that day about three thousand souls. And they held steadfastly to the apostles' teaching and fellowship, to the breaking of the bread and to the prayers" (Acts 2:41–42). This is as close to the very earliest days of Christianity as we can get.

"In Remembrance of Me"

From the very beginning, when the Christian Church began to be active in the world, its most important ceremony was the one Jesus had taught his disciples to do "in remembrance of me" (Luke 22:19). In fact, it would be tempting to see an outline of the Mass in Luke's description—"the apostles' teaching and fellowship" being the Liturgy of the Word, and "the breaking of bread" being the Eucharist. That might be reading too much into what Luke wrote, but we do certainly know that "the breaking of bread" was the distinctive Christian celebration from the very beginning of the Church.

We know that the Church was celebrating the Eucharist regularly by St. Paul's time. In his First Letter to the Corinthians, he recommends a back-to-basics approach. The Corinthians, he said, had been turning their celebrations into gluttonous feasts, where the rich stuffed themselves and the poor went hungry. "Don't you have houses for that?" Paul demands. "Let's not forget what the celebration really means."

> For I received from the Lord what I also delivered to you, that the Lord Jesus on the night when he was betrayed took bread, and when he had given thanks, he broke it, and said, "This is my body which is for you. Do this in remembrance of me." In the same way also the chalice, after supper, saying, "This chalice is the new covenant in my blood. Do this, as often as you drink it, in remembrance of me." For as often as you eat this bread and drink the chalice, you proclaim the Lord's death until he comes. (1 Corinthians 11:23–26)

This isn't just a commemoration, something the followers of Jesus do to think about him in an especially vivid way—the way we might raise a glass to a departed friend. It's something so powerful that it's a matter of life and death.

> Whoever, therefore, eats the bread or drinks the cup of the Lord in an unworthy manner will be guilty of profaning the body and blood of the Lord. Let a man examine himself, and so eat of the bread and drink of the cup. For any one who eats and drinks without discerning the body eats and drinks judgment upon himself. That is why many of you are weak and ill, and some have died. (1 Corinthians 11:27–30)

Misunderstanding the Eucharist can kill you: That's what Paul tells us. But for those who approach it in the right spirit, the Mass is heaven itself. The book of Revelation, in fact, paints heaven as a place where the liturgy goes on forever.

> Then I heard what seemed to be the voice of a great multitude, like the sound of many waters and like the sound of mighty thunderpeals, crying,
> "Hallelujah! For the Lord our God the Almighty reigns.

> Let us rejoice and exult and give him the glory,
>
> for the marriage of the Lamb has come,
>
> and his Bride has made herself ready;
>
> it was granted her to be clothed with fine linen, bright and
>
> pure"—
>
> for the fine linen is the righteous deeds of the saints.
>
> And the angel said to me, "Write this: Blessed are those who
> are invited to the marriage supper of the Lamb." And he said to
> me, "These are true words of God." (Revelation 19:6–9)

In heaven and earth the Eucharist is the center of the worship of the true God. St. Ignatius of Antioch, who wrote around the year 100, tells us that even the angels are condemned if they do not believe in the blood of Christ. The very mark of a heretic is disbelief in the Eucharist as truly the flesh of Christ.

> Don't deceive yourselves. Both the heavenly beings and the glorious angels, and rulers both visible and invisible, will be condemned if they do not believe in the blood of Christ....
>
> But think of those who hold different beliefs about the grace of Christ that has come to us—think how opposed they are to the will of God! They have no regard for love; they do not care for the widow, the orphan, or the oppressed; for the slave or for the free; for the hungry or for the thirsty.... They keep away from the Eucharist and from prayer, because they do not believe that the Eucharist is the flesh of our Savior Jesus Christ, who suffered for our sins, and whom the Father, out of his goodness, raised up again.
>
> The people who speak against this gift of God bring death on themselves by their arguments. It would be better if they would treat it with respect, so that they also might rise again.[1]

The Liturgy of the Eucharist was the part of the Mass that was open to the baptized only. Others were dismissed, and Christians were supposed to keep mum about the specifics of their ritual and doctrine. Naturally, strange rumors circulated among the pagans— terrible stories of human sacrifice, in which the Christians "ate flesh" and "drank blood." Pliny the Younger, who was a provincial governor around the time of St. Ignatius of Antioch, reported to the emperor Trajan that he had found these tales to be false.

> But they affirmed that their only guilt or error was that they usually met on a certain set day, before it was light, and sang a hymn to Christ in alternate verses, as they would to a god, and swore a solemn oath—not for any evil purpose, but never to commit any fraud, theft, or adultery, never to bear false witness, nor to deny a trust when they should be called on to hand it back. Afterward, they would disperse, and then come back together to eat—but to eat food of an ordinary and innocent sort.[2]

It's hard to interpret what Pliny is telling us, mostly because Pliny himself was completely ignorant of Christian belief and had no interest in learning about it, other than to answer the simple question of who was supposed to be killed for it. Some readers see Pliny's description as an indication that the Christians celebrated the Liturgy of the Word and the Liturgy of the Eucharist separately; on the other hand, Pliny could be describing a morning prayer in addition to the regular Mass. The way Pliny emphasizes the "ordinary and innocent" nature of the Christians' meal suggests that he was relieved to discover that the Christians consumed only a small amount of bread and wine and not the humans that the rumors reported.

Nevertheless, Pliny reinforces from a pagan point of view what we've already heard from Christian writers: that the Eucharist was the central ceremony of the Christian religion.

A Pure Sacrifice

To the Christians, of course—as we saw in St. Paul—the Eucharist was far more than a ceremony. It was the sacrifice the people of God offered in place of the old temple sacrifices. St. Irenaeus explains that this was the very thing the prophet Malachi had foretold: The temple priesthood would stop offering sacrifices, but a "pure" sacrifice to God would be offered "in every place."

> So when he gave his disciples directions to offer to God the first fruits of his own creation—not that he had need of them, but so that they themselves would be neither unfruitful nor ungrateful —he took bread, a created thing, and gave thanks, and said, "This is my body." And the cup as well, which is also part of that creation to which we belong, he proclaimed his blood. Thus he taught us the new offering of the covenant. The apostles passed it down to the Church, and the Church offers it to God throughout all the world—to the God who gives us the first fruits of his own gifts in the New Covenant for us to live on.
>
> This is what Malachi spoke about beforehand: "I have no pleasure in you, says the Lord of hosts, and I will not accept an offering from your hand. For from the rising of the sun to its setting my name is great among the nations, and in every place incense is offered to my name, and a pure offering; for my name is great among the nations, says the Lord of hosts" [Malachi 1:10–11].
>
> These words obviously mean that the people of old would indeed stop making offerings to God, but in every place sacrifice

shall be offered to him—a pure sacrifice—and his name is glorified among the nations.[3]

So what did this pure sacrifice look like? How did these very early Christians celebrate the Eucharist?

St. Hippolytus of Rome shows us that we would have been right at home in an early Christian Mass. Hippolytus wrote the Eucharistic Prayer most commonly used today, Eucharistic Prayer II in our current Roman Missal. The ancient text begins with familiar words and instructions.

> *The bishop, with the priests, prays alone. He puts on his shining garment, stands at the altar, and makes the sign of the cross on his forehead with his hand.*
>
> *Bishop.* The grace of Almighty God, and the love of our Lord Jesus Christ, and the fellowship of the Holy Spirit, be with you all.
>
> *Congregation.* And with your spirit.
>
> *Bishop.* Lift up your hearts.
>
> *Congregation.* We lift them up to the Lord.
>
> *Bishop.* Let us give thanks to the Lord.
>
> *Congregation.* It is meet and right to do so.
>
> *Bishop.* It is indeed meet and right...[4]

Hippolytus was writing in the early 200s, about eighteen hundred years ago. His contemporary, St. Cyprian, lived far away in North Africa but reports the very same words when he talks about the Mass: "The Lord be with you." "And with your spirit." "Lift up your hearts."[5]

Already around AD 150 St. Justin Martyr boasted that "there is not one single race of men … among whom prayers and Eucharist are not offered through the name of the crucified Jesus."[6] By that time the Mass may already have been diversified by language and culture. Yet it was still recognizable wherever Christians traveled. It was the universal sign of Christianity.

Archeologists have turned up very few crosses from that period and even fewer scraps of the Scriptures. But everywhere there were Christians in ancient times, we find images of the Mass, literary references to the Mass, symbols of the Mass. The sign of our religion remained the same, throughout the world and through the centuries.

Indeed, the Mass has kept its character even today, after ages and empires have come and gone. When the *Catechism of the Catholic Church*—published in 1994—describes a typical Sunday Mass in a typical modern parish, it does so in the words St. Justin used to describe the Roman Mass in the middle of the second century! (See *CCC*, 1345.)

While Christianity was still an illegal cult, while its leaders were hiding underground and regularly being dragged off to martyrdom, the Mass the Christians celebrated was, in all its essentials, the Mass we love today. The ancient words and gestures endure in Christian liturgies all over the world, and they always will.

CHAPTER TWO

Confession:
The History of Mercy

The sacrament of penance—reconciliation, confession—brings certain things to mind for Catholics today. A wooden booth at the back of the Church sports a red and a green light to indicate whether or not it's occupied. Inside the booth is a kneeler in front of a screen, behind which the priest sits. A prescribed formula allows us to express sorrow for our sins. Then comes Father's absolution in the name of God, and we go off to complete whatever penance he assigns.

Penance was very important to our earliest Christian ancestors. Though they did not use confessional boxes, they found comfort and healing in the sacrament. They performed sometimes heroic works of penance assigned by the Church. And they sought absolution of serious sins before they dared approach Holy Communion.

Early Christians testify to the importance of the sacrament, though perhaps not in the way we'd wish. We don't find descriptions of the rite, for example, or many images associated with its ancient practice. But this shouldn't surprise us: The sacraments functioned in the ancient Church the way major organs function in the body. They gave life. They sustained life. Most of the time people assumed their existence but didn't think about their functioning. We tend not to think about our liver or large intestine unless something has gone very wrong with it, and then we think only about the problem.

Thus, from the earliest times, the Fathers made many *allusions* to penance and even engaged in major controversies about its administration. But they tended to discuss problems and not the normal experience of the sacrament.

New Testament Origins

Like all the sacraments, penance has its roots in the New Testament. After his resurrection Jesus appeared to the disciples. "Jesus said to them again, 'Peace be with you. As the Father has sent me, even so I send you.' And when he had said this, he breathed on them, and said to them, 'Receive the Holy Spirit. If you forgive the sins of any, they are forgiven; if you retain the sins of any, they are retained'" (John 20:21–23; see also James 5:16).

Jesus breathed on the apostles and gave them the power to forgive sins and also to retain them—an awesome responsibility and one they saw as central to their mission. St. Paul saw his work as a "ministry of reconciliation" (2 Corinthians 5:18–19). The apostles passed this authority down to their successors, the bishops.

We have good evidence that the Church set down some formal guidelines for penance during that first generation, when the apostles were still its leaders. The *Didache* is a guidebook for the early Church whose liturgical portions probably date from no later than AD 48. If that date is right, then the *Didache* tells us what the Church was doing when many of the Twelve were still alive. You can't get much more apostolic than that. And already in the *Didache* we see that confession and Communion are intimately connected.

"Every Lord's day," says the guide, "gather, break bread, and give thanks—after you have confessed your sins, so that your sacrifice is pure. But no one who has a disagreement with his neighbor should come with you until the two of them have reconciled, so that your sacrifice is not profaned."[1]

Confession is the necessary prerequisite to Communion. And not only confession but also making things right. It's not enough to confess the sin: The sin has to stop, and the damage has to be undone.

That seems to have been the universal practice of the Church throughout the ages. We can recognize a familiar pastoral approach in the following beautiful exhortation to penance from the East.

A Healing Ministry

Aphrahat was a fourth-century bishop who lived in the Persian Empire, cut off by constant war from the rest of the Church in the Roman Empire. He spoke Syriac, a dialect of the same Aramaic language Jesus and his disciples spoke. In his book *On Penitents,* he urges every Christian who falls into sin to take the medicine the Church has prepared for him.

> There is a medicine for every disease, and when a skillful physician finds the medicine, the disease is healed.
>
> For those who are wounded in our battle, there is the medicine of penance, and those who put it on their wounds are healed. Physicians, you disciples of our wise Physician, take this medicine, and use it to heal the wounds of the sick.
>
> For warriors who are wounded in battle by someone who is fighting them find a skillful physician, and then they put themselves into his hands to be healed, so that he can make the wounded parts whole. And when a physician heals a man who was wounded in battle, the king gives him gifts and honors.

So, beloved, when someone is struggling in our battle, and the enemy fights against him and wounds him, it is appropriate to give him the medicine of penance, when the wounded man's repentance has grown great. For God does not reject the penitent: as Ezekiel the prophet said, "I have no pleasure in the death of the wicked, but that the wicked turn from his way and live."

Now, whoever is wounded in battle is not ashamed to put himself in the hands of a skillful physician, so that he can be healed of the wounds he received in battle. And the king does not reject a man who has been healed, but considers him part of his army again.

Likewise the man wounded by Satan should not be ashamed to confess his sin, and leave it behind, and beg for the medicine of penance. For gangrene comes if a man is ashamed to show his wound, and then the whole body is harmed. Whoever is not ashamed has his wound healed, and goes back to battle again; but if gangrene comes, he cannot be healed, and he cannot take up his arms again.

So for anyone who has been overcome in our battle, this is the way he can be healed: he can say, "I have sinned," and ask for penance. But whoever is ashamed cannot be healed, because he will not reveal to the physician who earns two pennies where his wounds are, so that the physician can heal all of them.[2]

Leniency Versus Severity

Aphrahat describes what was obviously the familiar practice of the Church in his time, even though his is one of the few explicit descriptions of it. Penance and absolution were available to anyone who truly repented. Everyone seems to have agreed that even a good Christian might fall into minor sins and that confession and atonement would get rid of the stain.

But what about the really big sins—the sins that are mortal? "All wrongdoing is sin, but there is sin which is not deadly" (1 John 5:17). Here's where the fights broke out.

Everyone agreed that the sins you had committed before you became a Christian were washed away. Christians enjoyed exchanging stories about what awful sinners they'd been before baptism "for the remission of sins" washed them clean and made them new creations. Was it possible to repent of sins after that?

Some said no. The *Shepherd of Hermas*, a second-century book that some local churches revered as Scripture, refused repentance to the baptized. As a special privilege Hermas gave each person *one chance* at sacramental confession, but that's it.

In the book Hermas, a former slave, reported visions in which he interrogated an angel about many things, repentance being one of them.

> And I said, "Sir, I have heard some teachers say that the only repentance is the one that happens when we go down into the water and receive remission of the sins we committed before."
>
> He said to me, "Yes, that was sound teaching you heard, for what they said was true. Anyone who has received remission of sins should not sin any more, but live a pure life.... There is no repentance for sins for those who believe now, or who will believe in the future; they have only remission of their previous sins. The Lord has given repentance to those who were called before our time.... So I tell you, that if anyone is tempted by the devil and sins after that great, holy calling by which the Lord has called his people to life eternal, he has only one chance to repent. If he sins frequently after that, and then repents, his repentance is no use to him; it will be hard for him to live."[3]

Many Christians thought otherwise. The question became especially important in times of persecution—or rather immediately after times of persecution.

Finding a Balance

Roman persecutions were insanely reasonable affairs. Usually the persecuting officials gave Christians every opportunity to renounce their illegal faith. Just a small sacrifice to the emperor's genius, and the charges would be dropped, the tortures would stop, and the ex-Christian could walk away free. Many Christians broke down under torture and made the pagan sacrifices their tormentors demanded.

When the persecution abated, many of those lapsed Christians were sincerely ashamed of what they had done and wanted to come back into the Church. What was to be done with them?

Rigorists said that lapsed Christians could *never* be forgiven, or they followed *Hermas* in saying that *only one* grave sin could be forgiven. The second-century African author Tertullian (who counted *Hermas* as Scripture) was one of the most eloquent champions of the rigorists. He explained that Satan is constantly throwing temptations in the way of Christians, hoping to gain back what was lost to him by their baptism.

> Since God foresaw these poisons of his, even though the gate of forgiveness has been shut and locked with the bolt of baptism, God allows it to be opened a little. In the vestibule he has put a second repentance, so that the gate may be opened for those who knock. But this time the repentance is once and for all, because now it is for the second time. It can never happen again, because the first repentance was in vain.
>
> Was not even that first repentance enough? You have what you showed you did not deserve, because you lost what you had been

given. If the Lord is lenient enough to give you a way to get back what you lost, be thankful for that benefit—a greater benefit than the first. For restoring is greater than giving, since having lost a thing is worse than never having received it at all.[4]

Later Tertullian came to believe that he had been too lenient. Leaving the Catholic Church behind, he fell in with the ultra-rigorist Montanists. When Pope Callixtus declared that the Church would forgive adultery and fornication after penance, Tertullian responded that grave sins were beyond the power of the Church to forgive.[5]

On the opposite end of the spectrum, some priests were willing to let the lapsed back into communion right away, assuring them that everything was all right. This was also heresy. For the Church forgives sins, but she does not ignore them.

Between these two extremes were the sensible moderates—the men who helped the Church refine the orthodox doctrine of penance. Cyprian of Carthage was one of them. He was a third-century bishop of North Africa, where persecutions had been exceptionally strong. Africa produced more than its fair share of both the rigorists and the anything-goes types.

In dealing with the latter, Cyprian was always careful not to fall into the errors of the former. True repentance was possible and should be encouraged. But Cyprian worried that, if he made it too easy for the lapsed to come back into communion with the Church, he might deny them the chance for true repentance. They had been wounded by their sin; they could be cured only by long and difficult repentance, not by a pat on the back and a soothing reassurance.

But how can they really feel sorrow and repent, when some of the priests block their groans and tears by letting them come right back into communion? Those priests do not know that it is written, "Those who call you happy mislead you, and destroy the path of your feet."[6]

So of course our healthy and true advice is unsuccessful. The truth that would benefit them is blocked by wicked, tempting flattery.

Instead, the wounded and diseased minds of the lapsed suffer the same things those who are sick in the body often suffer. Wholesome food and drink disgust them; they crave things that seem pleasing and sweet for the moment. They invite harm and death by their rashness and self-indulgence. And as long as the sweet temptation is deceiving them with its delights, the skillful physician's true medicine cannot help them.

You, therefore, should take the advice in my letters about this, faithfully and wholesomely. Do not retreat from better advice. And take care to read my letters to my colleagues as well, if any of them are there, or if any come to you. In that way, united in agreement, we can stick to a healthy plan for soothing and healing the wounds of the lapsed, with a plan for dealing with them in detail when, by the Lord's mercy, we can meet together.

Meanwhile, if any impulsive hothead, either among our priests and deacons or among strangers, should dare to commune with the lapsed before our decree, he should be excommunicated, and he can make excuses for his foolishness when (Lord willing) we meet in assembly again.[7]

Cyprian was a moderate: It's important for us to remember that. He wasn't saying the lapsed could never come back into communion with the Church, the way some of the extremists (like Tertullian and Hippolytus) were saying. On the other hand, he wasn't willing to say their apostasy didn't matter. They could come back, but it was going to cost them. Their repentance had to be real, and it would take a while to erase the blot.

These are the treacherous straits the Church has always had to navigate. On the one side are the fanatics who will not forgive; on the other side are the easygoing indifferentists who shrug off any sin, no matter how scandalous. Somewhere in the middle is the true Christian doctrine of penance—with the true Christian practice of sacramental confession. Cyprian did his best to keep the Church from hitting the rocks.

By our standards Cyprian might seem severe sometimes. But he left the door open for mercy when the fanatics would slam and bolt it, and that puts him in the orthodox current.

Public Confession, Public Penance

Was confession public or private in the early Church?

From the documents it seems likely that sins that affected the social order (adultery, theft, or rape, for example) were confessed publicly, at least early on. We can only imagine what a deterrent this was to sin. But it could also be a big deterrent to confession. A man who confessed in public to adultery implicated not only himself but also his partner in sin. Confessing a rape publicly might elicit forgiveness for the perpetrator but also subject the victim to shame.

We can see then why the Church gradually moved toward private confession—removing the fear of public exposure but firmly holding to the doctrine that penance is necessary for communion. Nevertheless, in the ancient Church as in the modern, public scandal sometimes meant public excommunication and public penance, no matter how prominent the sinner. Probably the most dramatic example involved an emperor.

Theodosius the Great was the last Roman emperor to rule the whole empire, east and west. In general Christian historians have regarded him as one of the good guys. He suppressed the last remnants of official pagan religion, and for a while it almost seemed as though he might succeed in restoring the ancient glory of Rome but on a Christian footing.

But Theodosius was not without his faults. When his governor in Thessalonica was assassinated in AD 390, Theodosius threw a tantrum that ended in the indiscriminate massacre of seven thousand residents of the city. Ambrose, bishop of Milan (which by then had replaced Rome as the administrative capital), responded by refusing Communion to the emperor. Legend—probably amplified for dramatic effect—has Ambrose blocking Theodosius' path as the emperor tried to enter the church.

At any rate Ambrose wrote Theodosius a private letter in which he persuaded the emperor that, after such a glaring public crime, he needed to make an equally public penance before he could receive absolution. With another emperor that letter might have cost Ambrose his life. Theodosius, however, submitted to the judgment of the bishop. In the end Theodosius had to go through a long and very public penance before Ambrose would lift his excommunication. The emperor laid aside all the insignia of power and lamented his sin in the church, where everyone could see.

This made a powerful impression on the people: The emperor himself was setting the example of penance. It was not just a political stunt. Ambrose seems to have reached Theodosius' conscience and made a real impression on him. By all accounts—including the account of Ambrose, who delivered Theodosius' funeral oration years later—the emperor's contrition was sincere. "For the rest of his life," Ambrose remembered, "not a day went by when he did not grieve for his error."[8]

For his part Theodosius seems to have understood that Ambrose had shown him real Christian love—the love that sometimes prescribes bitter medicine to cure a deadly case of sin. "I don't know of any bishop worthy of the name," Theodosius said after his penance was all over, "except Ambrose."[9]

From the Scriptures to the Bible

The Bible is the world's favorite book. It's the all-time best-seller, available in every major language and most minor languages. In English alone we can choose from an alphabet soup of versions: *NAB, RSV-CE, JB, NJB, NIV, KJV, CEV, NKJV*, and so on.

They're all big books. The word *Bible* means simply "The Book." Colloquially we call it "The Good Book." So it's natural that we think of the Scriptures as a single bound volume.

The earliest Christians, however, would not have thought of the Bible that way. Though they knew its contents intimately, they could not encounter it as we do. How did they encounter it? To answer that question we have to imagine a world quite different from our own.

Christianity arose in a world with no electronic media and no printing presses. These technologies hadn't been imagined, never mind invented. Literary culture was important, but it was available to few. Only the wealthy could afford to have documents copied by hand. The process was labor-intensive, time-consuming, and very expensive. Education was a luxury anyway, and most people could not read much beyond the familiar words on the signs in the marketplace.

From the beginning Christians held certain documents as authoritative. Yet even these did not circulate as a book. Local churches possessed whatever documents they had the cash and the opportunity to pull together. A bishop might own one or two of the Gospels and some of the letters of St. Paul. Only the most fortunate churches could possess most of the books we now know as the Old Testament and the New Testament.

Whatever texts the local church possessed, ordinary Christians encountered when they went to Mass. Around AD 155 St. Justin Martyr described the first part of a typical Mass in the city of Rome: "And on the day called Sunday, all who live in cities or in the country gather together to one place, and the memoirs of the apostles or the writings of the prophets are read, as long as time permits. Then, when the reader has ceased, the presider teaches, and urges the imitation of these good things."[1]

From Justin's description we see that, at a very early date, the Church limited which books could be read at Mass. It couldn't be just any book or even any Christian book. St. Justin specifies (in terms an outsider could understand) that acceptable books were "the memoirs of the apostles or the writings of the prophets."

For us this raises an important question: How did the Christians, dispersed throughout the world, know which books were acceptable for public proclamation and which were not?

It's not something they could discover by going to a bookstore. They had to consult the Church, and the Church deliberated carefully before drawing together all those good books into a single Good Book.

What the Old Testament Means to a Christian

Of course, the Christians of the first generation agreed upon the special status of the Scriptures of ancient Judaism, "the law of Moses and the prophets and the psalms" (Luke 24:45). It was these Scriptures that St. Paul described as "inspired by God and profitable for teaching, for reproof, for correction, and for training in righteousness" (2 Timothy 3:16).

In that first generation—that first light of the gospel—Paul's probable disciple, St. Clement of Rome, said that "holy Scriptures …are true…[and] were given through the Holy Spirit; and…nothing unrighteous or counterfeit is written in them."[2] That is the greatest possible reverence, the greatest possible trust.

Even so, the *meaning* of these Scriptures was controversial. Christians debated with Jews, for example, about how to interpret the writings that Christians said belonged to the "old covenant"— the books held sacred by the people of God as they awaited the Messiah. St. Justin Martyr spent much of his *Dialogue With Trypho* going over exactly that debate.

In the dialogue Trypho is an educated Jew who engages Justin in a lively but friendly debate. Justin is honest enough not to paint the encounter as a triumph for himself: Trypho walks away unconvinced of the Christian argument. But the two part as friends, which is the way all such debates should end.

One of Trypho's arguments is that the Messiah is supposed to come from the loins of David, whereas the Christians say Jesus was born of a virgin.

> *Trypho:* So why does the Word say to David, that out of his loins God shall take to Himself a Son, and shall establish His kingdom, and shall set Him on the throne of His glory (2 Samuel 7:12–13)?
>
> *Justin:* Trypho, if Isaiah's prophecy, "Behold, a virgin shall conceive," were spoken, not to the house of David, but to one of the

other twelve tribes, then perhaps this might be a hard question to answer. But since this prophecy refers to the house of David, Isaiah is explaining how what God spoke to David in mystery will happen. But perhaps you didn't realize, friend, that many sayings were written in a hidden or roundabout way, or mysteriously, and there were many symbolic acts, all of which were only explained by prophets who lived after the people who said or did them.

Trypho: Of course.[3]

Having won that much from Trypho, Justin proceeds to open up an argument that looks strikingly modern. It seems that Trypho's Jewish teachers argued that the prophecies applied not to Jesus Christ but to various historical figures of the past. More than that, they were beginning to reject the Septuagint, the Greek translation of the Hebrew Scriptures made centuries before the time of Christ. Some of its translations seemed to favor the Christian side of the debate.

Justin: So if I can show you that this prophecy of Isaiah refers to our Christ, and not (as you say) to Hezekiah, then won't I once again force you not to believe your teachers when they venture to say that the interpretation of the seventy elders under King Ptolemy of Egypt is wrong in some places?

For when some passages in the Scriptures seem to contradict them explicitly and prove that their opinions are wrong, they say those passages weren't really written that way at all. But when they think they can distort the passages to refer to human actions, then they say that those passages refer, not to our own Jesus Christ, but to whomever they decide.

So, for example, they have taught you that the passage we were talking about refers to Hezekiah—and, as I promised, I'm about to prove them wrong.

And since they have no choice, they agree that some of the Scriptures we bring up, which expressly prove that Christ was to suffer and to be worshiped as God (the passages I already recited to you), really do refer to Christ. But they go on to say that this man is not Christ. But they do admit that he will come to suffer, and to reign, and to be worshiped, and to be God. So I'll show you that this opinion is just as silly as the others.[4]

For Christians the meaning of the Old Testament is obvious. The whole thing, from start to finish, points toward the coming of Christ. Christians and Jews could have lively debates precisely because they recognized the same Scriptures. Later on rabbinic Judaism rejected some of the books of the Old Testament—the same ones Protestants reject now. But in the time of the early Church, the Septuagint was the standard for Christians and Greek-speaking Jews alike.

The Four Gospels

For Christ and his first apostles, *Scripture* meant the Old Testament. Even the earliest New Testament books wouldn't be written till more than a decade after Jesus ascended into heaven.

What the apostles did have was their vivid memories of what Christ had taught. They had spent three years following him, listening to everything he said, and—just as important—watching everything he did. That intensive training was what prepared them to take his message to the four corners of the earth.

But as the apostles grew older and many of them faced martyrdom, their successors had to prepare to continue to spread the Good News. It would be very useful to have a written record of what the apostles remembered, because no one else had had that intensive training with the Master himself. So the apostles and their close disciples began to write down their memories of what Jesus had done and said.

Eusebius, the Church historian of Constantine's time, quotes Clement of Alexandria on the origin of the Gospel of Mark, which is a very interesting passage because it comes from someone who lived in the city where, according to ancient tradition, St. Mark lived as a bishop and died a martyr.

> This is how the Gospel according to Mark came about. Peter had been preaching the Word publicly at Rome, and telling the Gospel by the Spirit. Many of his audience asked that Mark, who had followed him for a long time and remembered his sayings, should write them out. So he wrote his Gospel and gave it to the people who had asked for it. When Peter heard about it, he neither directly prohibited it nor encouraged it.[5]

It seems that many writers took up the challenge of gospel writing. Luke, who wrote when many—perhaps most—of the apostles were still alive, suggests that he writes his account precisely because so many other people have already written theirs:

> Inasmuch as many have undertaken to compile a narrative of the things which have been accomplished among us, just as they were delivered to us by those who from the beginning were eye-witnesses and ministers of the word, it seemed good to me also, having followed all things closely for some time past, to write an orderly account for you, most excellent Theophilus, that you may know the truth concerning the things of which you have been informed. (Luke 1:1–4)

Short as it is, we learn several things from Luke's little dedicatory epistle. First, for example, we learn that "many" wrote accounts of the life of Jesus. Second, we learn that eyewitness accounts were their main sources. Third, we know that Theophilus had already heard the story of the gospel but probably had not heard an "orderly" account.

Of those many lives of Jesus that were written, however, we have only four. (There are other "gospels," like the Gospel of Thomas and the Gospel of Peter, but textual scholars almost universally agree that they were written much later than Luke's Gospel.) It seems that these four Gospels very quickly established themselves as the only reliable ones.

St. Irenaeus of Lyons wrote a comprehensive treatise against all the heresies he could think of—including the ones that claimed alternative "gospels." He wrote this sometime in the 180s, when Christianity was still an illegal, underground cult as far as the imperial government was concerned. Here he argues that the number four is a symbolically fitting number of Gospels:

> It is impossible for there to be more or fewer Gospels than there are. For there are four parts of the world we live in, and four major winds. So while the Church is scattered throughout the whole world, and the "pillar and bulwark" [1 Timothy 3:15] of the Church is the Gospel and Spirit of life, it is appropriate that she should have four pillars, breathing immortality in every direction, and giving us new life.
>
> From these things, it is obvious that the Word, the Creator of all, who sits upon the Cherubim and contains all things, who was made manifest to humanity, has given us the Gospel in four different ways, but all bound together by the same Spirit.[6]

Irenaeus's explanation of why there are four Gospels probably wouldn't be taken seriously by most modern biblical scholars. But it does show us that, well before the year 200, the idea that there were only four was so entrenched in the Catholic Church that it seemed like part of the order of nature. Heretics might be peddling their alternative gospels, as indeed they do today, but for the great majority of orthodox Christians, there were only four. This had already been true for a while by Irenaeus's time—and remember that Irenaeus wrote more than a hundred years before Constantine, the emperor who made Christianity legal in the Roman Empire.

Shaping the New Testament

The rest of the New Testament was also pretty much settled in the time of Irenaeus, with the exception of a few of the books toward the end. Jude, for example, was disputed; some accepted it as Scripture, some not. On the other hand, there were some who would include the *Shepherd of Hermas* and the Letter of Barnabas. But on the whole the New Testament looked very much the same to a Christian of the 100s as it looks to us in the 2000s.

Eusebius cites some otherwise lost works of St. Clement of Alexandria to show what he considered Scripture:

> To sum up briefly, Clement…gives us summaries of all canonical Scripture, including the disputed books (by which I mean Jude and the other Catholic epistles, Barnabas, and the so-called Apocalypse of Peter).
>
> He says that the Epistle to the Hebrews is the work of Paul, and that it was written to the Hebrews in Hebrew. But Luke translated it carefully and published it for the Greeks, which is why we find the same style of language in this epistle and in the Acts.

> But he says that it does not begin with the words "Paul the
> Apostle" because the Hebrews were prejudiced against him and
> did not trust him, so he wisely decided not to put them off right
> from the start by giving his name.[7]

By the time the Church got around to listing an official canon of the
New Testament, the canon was already in place. A fragment, called
the *Muratorian Canon*, survives from the second century; it contains
most of the final list of the New Testament, with some additional
books that were later rejected. St. Athanasius, in the mid–fourth
century, published a list that is identical with the New Testament as
we know it today.

The official proclamation of the New Testament canon was really
only a confirmation of what everyone in the Catholic Church
already knew and already proclaimed in the readings of the Mass.
The matter was settled with the Synods of Hippo (AD 393) and
Carthage (397 and 419), which were guided by St. Augustine.
These synods confirmed the list of a Roman synod of 382, which
had been attended by St. Jerome and presided over by Pope St.
Damasus. This list filtered out over time to the extremities of
Christianity.

Even while the canon of the New Testament was under debate, a
debate opened up on a second front. Was the Old Testament really
part of Christian Scripture?

New Testament, New God?

We've mentioned that the Mass was the ordinary place for proclamation of the Scriptures. It was also the ordinary place for their
interpretation. The Church Fathers were preachers and pastors pri-
marily, not academics. They made no distinction between changing
someone's mind and changing his heart and his life.

Biblical interpretation, moreover, belonged not to individuals but to the Church. This was the clear teaching of the apostles: "First of all you must understand this, that no prophecy of Scripture is a matter of one's own interpretation" (2 Peter 1:20). The Fathers held fast to that tradition. A disciple of the apostle John, St. Polycarp of Smyrna, wrote around AD 110: "If anyone interprets the words of the Lord according to his own perverse inclinations and says there is no resurrection or judgment, he is the firstborn of Satan. Let's do away with the vanity of the crowd and their false doctrines, and let's return to the word that has been handed down to us from the beginning."[8]

Polycarp, however, would live to see the rise of a biblical interpreter just so perversely inclined and with the smarts, the money, and the eloquence to draw an immense crowd to himself. His name was Marcion, and he was a shipbuilder with a vast fortune.

St. Irenaeus, who was a disciple of Polycarp, recalled that his master had once encountered Marcion on the streets of Rome. Marcion said to the elderly bishop, "Don't you know who I am?"

And Polycarp invoked his own definition of a Christian who would dare to use private judgment against the biblical interpretation of the Church. He said, "Of course I recognize the firstborn of Satan."[9]

The heresy of Marcion denied that the Old Testament had anything to do with Christians. The God of the Old Testament was not our God, Marcion said, though that God had created the world. Marcion's "Christ" had come to reveal a new God. St. Paul's preaching about freedom from the Law meant that we were to turn our backs on "the old God" of the Jews.

This is actually a heresy that comes up again and again throughout history. People who find it hard to deal with the Jewish origins of Christianity try to find some way to drive a wedge between Christians and Jews. Wouldn't it be so much easier, they say, if we didn't have to believe any of that stuff in the Old Testament?

We'll let the theologian Tertullian, who shortly after the year 200 wrote a long book against the Marcionite heresy, explain the heresy and point out the immediate logical problem with it:

> Marcion's main business, and his characteristic one, is separating the Law and the Gospel. His disciples will tell you that this is their very best reason for having taken up his heresy, and for sticking with it. Marcion's *Antitheses,* or contradictory statements, attempt to show that the Gospel is different from the Law. The argument is that, because the two are so different, there must be two different gods.
>
> Because the opposition between the Law and the Gospel is exactly what supposedly makes it clear that the God of the Gospel is different from the God of the Law, the God who was made known by that difference obviously could not have been known beforehand. That means he could not have been revealed by Christ, who came before there was a difference, but must have been made up by Marcion, who created this breach of the peace between the Gospel and the Law. This peace, which had remained undamaged and unshaken from the time Christ appeared to the time of Marcion's audacious doctrine, was doubtless kept precisely by the belief that the God of both Law and Gospel was none other than the Creator—the Creator whom Marcion has separated from the God of the Gospel after such a long time.[10]

Tertullian argued that you could easily prove Marcion's opinions were absurd from St. Paul's writings. Pay special attention to what

Tertullian tells us about how to discover which teachings are truly "apostolic."

> Now if [Paul] was so eager to put aside the law of the old God because he wanted to preach a new God, why doesn't [he] give us any rule about the new God? All he talks about is the old law. Obviously, we were still supposed to have faith in the Creator; it was only his law that was coming to an end....
>
> Look, if Paul had been preaching another God, there couldn't be any question of whether the law was to be kept or not. The law wouldn't belong to the new lord, who was inimical to the law. Just the fact that the God was new and different would get rid of any question about the old law, which was foreign to him—in fact, Paul wouldn't even mention it.
>
> But instead, the whole question Paul had to deal with was that, although the God of the law was the same God Christ preached, yet Christ preached against the law. Obviously, faith in the Creator and his Christ remained. The only things that changed were the way we lived and the rules we obeyed.
>
> Some people raised questions about sacrifices to idols. Others asked about whether women had to be veiled. Still others asked about marriage and divorce. Some even asked about the resurrection. But no one argued about God.
>
> Now, if that question had come up at all, surely the apostle would have mentioned it. Doubtless the pure belief in God suffered some corruption after the time of the apostles, but just as certainly the teaching of the apostles on this one great point never wavered while they were alive.
>
> Plainly, the only teaching we can call "apostolic" is the one that's still taught at the churches founded by the apostles. But

you won't find any church of apostolic origin that doesn't put its Christian faith in the Creator. If those churches are corrupt, where will we find the pure ones? Will we find them among the enemies of the Creator? Go ahead—show us how one of your churches can trace its line back to an apostle, and you'll win the argument.

So since it's obvious in every way that there was no other God in our religion from the time of Christ down to the time of Marcion, we've proved our point well enough. We've shown that the "god" of our heretic first became known by his separation of the gospel and the law. That proves what we said before, which is that we can't believe in any "god" that a man makes up out of his own imagination—unless that man is a prophet, in which case his own imagination has nothing to do with the case. But if Marcion is an inspired prophet, he's got to prove it. We can't have any hemming and hawing.

No, all heresy is pushed out by this wedge of truth: Christ, as we've proved, revealed no other God but the Creator.[11]

Origen, writing in the early 200s, tells us that the Old Testament and the New Testament are equally the Word of God, and the Word of God is Christ. Thus Christ is just as much found in the Old Testament as in the New:

All who believe and are certain that grace and truth come to us through Jesus Christ, and who know that Christ is truth—as he himself declared: "I am the truth"—have that knowledge that prompts us to good and happy lives from the words and teaching of Christ himself. And by "words of Christ" we do not mean only the words he spoke when he became man and inhabited the flesh. No, before that time, Christ, the Word of God, was in

Moses and the Prophets. Without the Word of God, how would they have been able to prophesy about Christ?

If we were not trying to keep this work as brief as possible, we could easily prove this statement from the Holy Scriptures— namely, that Moses or the prophets said and did everything they did because they were filled with the Spirit of Christ.[12]

Apostolic Authority

We just saw the standard Tertullian used to measure what was orthodox: "the only teaching we can call 'apostolic' is the one that's still taught at the churches founded by the apostles." The apostolic tradition is what gives the Church the right to decide what is Scripture and what isn't. The Marcionites didn't have that tradition, so they didn't have that right.

We see that standard applied again when we come to Tertullian's more detailed discussion of which of the Christian books count as "Scripture."

> So, then, it is obvious that the things that are earlier are truer, *if* the earlier things come from the very beginning, *if* what comes from the beginning comes from the apostles themselves. If that is so, then it will certainly be just as obvious that what comes from the apostles is what has been kept as a sacred deposit in the churches of the apostles.
>
> Let us see what milk the Corinthians drank from Paul— which rule of faith corrected the Galatians; what the Philippians, Thessalonians, Ephesians make of it; what the Romans have to say, the Romans who were so close to the apostles, to whom Peter and Paul together left the Gospel sealed with their own blood. We have also the churches Saint John fostered—for, though Marcion rejects his *Revelation,* we can still trace the line of the

bishops of those churches back to John. And we can find the illustrious founders of the other churches in the same way.

I tell you, then, that this Gospel of Luke, which we are defending with all our might, has been accepted in them since it was first published. And not only in those churches, but also in all the churches united with them in the communion of the Gospel of Christ. Marcion's gospel, on the other hand, is unknown to most people, and those who do know it condemn it. Of course, it has its churches too, but they are peculiarly its own—as recent as they are bogus. If you want to know their source, you will sooner find apostasy than apostolicity in it: Marcion himself was their founder, or one of his swarm of followers. Even wasps make hives, and likewise these Marcionites make churches.

The same authority of the apostolic churches will vouch for the other Gospels as well—that is, John and Matthew—while we may declare that the Gospel Mark published belonged to Peter, with Mark as his interpreter.[13]

Here, incidentally, Tertullian has rattled off a list of New Testament Scripture that includes most of the major letters of Paul, the four Gospels, and the book of Revelation. He's not trying to give us a complete list of the canonical books, but his casual references confirm once again that the New Testament in his time already had a shape very similar to the one we're familiar with.

Though the Marcionite heresy keeps popping up in various forms, from the point of view of the Catholic Church it never made much of an impression. It did render us one important service though: It forced the Church to be explicit about the place of the Old Testament in the canon—to say, beyond possibility of misinterpretation, that the Old Testament was just as much part of the Scriptures as the New Testament.

Still there was a lingering question. Which version of the Scriptures was Scripture?

Treasured and Treacherous Translations

Christianity began in Palestine, where Aramaic was the everyday language. But because Palestine was part of the Roman Empire, most people there also spoke Greek, which was the language of trade and business throughout the East. As soon as you moved beyond Palestine, Greek was the language you had to know. That's why all the Christian Scriptures were written in Greek and why the Septuagint was the Christians' favorite translation of the Old Testament.

Even in the Latin-speaking West, you could take it for granted that most educated people could read Greek. (But very few could read Hebrew.) And the Church wasn't supposed to be just for educated people. Ordinary believers should hear the Word of God in their own language, and in the West ordinary believers spoke Latin.

The Septuagint had been the standard Greek translation of the Old Testament since the beginning of the Church. It was regarded with the same reverence that some Christians in America feel toward the older English translations of the Bible. There were strong arguments, for example, that the Septuagint represented an early, pure text tradition that had been corrupted in later Hebrew editions. And the Septuagint was the version cited by the apostles themselves as they composed the New Testament.

Some Christians regarded the Septuagint as divinely inspired in itself, not just a translation of divinely inspired Scripture. St. Irenaeus repeats a popular legend about the seventy scholars who worked on the Septuagint:

Before the Romans took over their kingdom, while the Macedonians still had Asia, Ptolemy son of Lagus, eager to adorn his library in Alexandria with a collection of all the worthwhile books in the world, sent a request to the people of Jerusalem that they should have their Scriptures translated into Greek. (At that time the people of Jerusalem were still under Macedonian rule.)

So they sent seventy of their elders, who were fluent in the Scriptures and in both languages, to do what Ptolemy had asked.

But Ptolemy wanted to test them. He was afraid that they might conspire together to hide the truth about the Scriptures by falsifying the translation. So he separated them, and ordered each one to make the same translation of all the books. But when they all were gathered together before Ptolemy and compared their translations, God was certainly glorified, and it was proved that the Scriptures were divine. For each one read out the translation in exactly the same words, from beginning to end. Even the Gentiles present could see that the Scriptures had been translated by the inspiration of God.[14]

With such a reputation the Septuagint was fairly secure as the Church's official translation. Nevertheless, in the Latin-speaking West, many books of the Bible were translated into the language of the ordinary people. Some of those Latin translations were better than others, and they all had problems.

What was needed was a great scholar to take on the task of providing a reliable Latin translation. And that scholar was St. Jerome.

Of all the Fathers, the one we associate most with the Bible is St. Jerome, because his translation is still the standard against which other Catholic translations are compared. A man of deep and broad learning, he was also one who didn't suffer fools gladly. He was notoriously hard to get along with. If he thought someone was wrong, he said so without mincing words and probably threw in a few personal insults while he was at it.

When, at the pope's request, Jerome translated the Old Testament into Latin, he insisted on going back to the Hebrew—angering many Christians who had used the Septuagint all these years and refused to accept any deviation from it. Who was Jerome to take it upon himself to revise the Bible?

Jerome was ready with a response:

> At every step in my work on the books of Holy Scripture, I have to answer the abuse of my opponents, who charge that my translation is some sort of insult to the translators of the Septuagint....
>
> So listen up, you raving critics. My motive in slaving away at this book was not to reproach the old translation, but to shed a little light on the passages in it that are obscure, or have been left out, or perhaps have been corrupted by the copyists. I have a little knowledge of Hebrew, and, as for Latin, I've spent my whole life, almost from the cradle, among grammarians, rhetoricians, and philosophers.
>
> Since the Septuagint was published—and even now, when the light of Christ's Gospel is shining abroad—the Judaizing heretics Aquila, Symmachus, and Thedotion have been welcomed by the Greeks. These heretics have hidden many of the mysteries of salvation by their lying translations. And yet, through the Hexapla [an early edition of the Bible that placed six different versions in parallel columns], they're found in the churches and preached on by the clergy.
>
> But I am a Christian, born of Christian parents, carrying the banner of the Cross on my forehead. I've been eager to recover what is lost, correct what has been corrupted, and unveil the

mysteries of the Church in pure and faithful language. Shouldn't I be in a much better position than those heretics to escape the condemnation of picky or malicious readers?

If you like, you can keep your old books, with their purple pages full of gold and silver letters—"uncial" letters, as they call them. They may be stacks of pretty writing rather than real books, but you can have them—if you'll leave me and my friends our poor pages and copies, not beautiful but accurate.

I've worked hard to translate both the Greek Septuagint and the Hebrew text, which is the basis of mine, into Latin. You can pick the version you like, but you'll find that what you object to in me comes from sound scholarship, not malice.[15]

Jerome was indeed cranky and angry. He was usually the smartest person in the room, and he knew it, and he had no patience with people who thought they were smarter when they weren't.

But perhaps Jerome's abrasive personality was just what the Church needed at that particular moment in history. Translation is a difficult task that usually wins the translator more enemies than friends. The Italians say now, as they did in the time of Jerome, *traduttore, traditore*—a translator is a traitor. The Talmud is even more to the point as it describes the translator's dilemma: "He who translates a verse verbatim is a liar. But he who alters it is a villain and a heretic."[16]

Jerome was the kind of guy who was ready for the inevitable match of name-calling. His uncompromising scholarship demanded that he consult the Hebrew. And the pope approved, though he also insisted that Jerome translate from Greek the texts for which Jerome could find no Hebrew originals, such as the books of Sirach, Maccabees, Judith, Tobit, Wisdom, and parts of the book of Daniel.

In the end Jerome produced a masterpiece of a translation—still the gold standard for the Catholic Bible. And his short fuse made it a lot easier to agree with him than to disagree with him.

Today most English versions of the Bible are translated from the original languages—a practice of which St. Jerome would doubtless have approved. But the official translation of the Church is still Jerome's version, with careful revisions that reflect important discoveries by modern scholars. We call it the Vulgate, meaning the "common version."

The Saints in Heaven: Stones Cry Out

Once when Jesus' disciples were raising a ruckus with their prayers of praise and thanksgiving, people complained about the noise. Jesus answered the critics: "I tell you, if these were silent, the very stones would cry out" (Luke 19:40).

Well, there's nothing silent about the early Church's witness to the doctrine of the communion of saints. It appears often in the documents we have from that period. It remains with us in the prayers and liturgies our spiritual ancestors have left us.

Still, even the stones *do* cry out. If you take a tour around the city of Rome and visit the places where the martyrs and popes were laid to rest, you'll see graffiti and inscriptions dating back to the third century. Some are roughly scrawled and full of misspellings; some are carefully chiseled and rendered as poetry. They represent prayers that rose from pilgrims and mourners. They are pleas for saintly intercession.

> *Paul and Peter, pray for Victor!*
> *I commend to St. Basilla the innocent Gemellus.*
> *Anatolias, . . . intercede for your sister.*
> *Pray for your brothers and your friends.*

Pray for your parents.
Martyrs and saints, keep Maria in mind.
O Hippolytus, remember Peter, a sinner.
Master Crescentio, heal my eyes for me!
O St. Sixtus, remember Aurelius Repentinus in your prayers!
O holy souls, remember Marcianus, Successus, Severus, and all our
  brethren!

The invocation of the saints is a practice that dates to earliest times. Christians knew then, as they know now, that the saints of the past surround us. All who ever died still live, as Cardinal John Henry Newman said. And the blessed don't stop caring about us because they're having so much fun in heaven. On the contrary, their charity is perfected in heaven, and they have all the time in the world to indulge it.

The God of the Living

In Jesus' time there were Jews who denied the afterlife altogether. The Sadducees were strict empiricists. They believed in what they saw and nothing more. So they denied the possibility of resurrection and the existence of a spiritual component in human beings (see Acts 23:8). They believed that death was the end, and they were ready to debate Jesus with a clever little thought experiment.

> The same day Sadducees came to him, who say that there is no resurrection; and they asked him a question, saying, "Teacher, Moses said, 'If a man dies, having no children, his brother must marry the widow, and raise up children for his brother.' Now there were seven brothers among us; the first married, and died, and having no children left his wife to his brother. So too the second and third, down to the seventh. After them all, the woman

died. In the resurrection, therefore, to which of the seven will she be wife? For they all had her."

But Jesus answered them, "You are wrong, because you know neither the Scriptures nor the power of God. For in the resurrection they neither marry nor are given in marriage, but are like angels in heaven. And as for the resurrection of the dead, have you not read what was said to you by God, 'I am the God of Abraham, and the God of Isaac, and the God of Jacob'? He is not God of the dead, but of the living." And when the crowd heard it, they were astonished at his teaching. (Matthew 22:23–33)

As usual Jesus didn't wriggle out of a clever intellectual trap; he took the opportunity to teach us something profound, in this case about the resurrection. Abraham, Isaac, and Jacob are still with us. The saints of old are alive, for God is the God of the living. Three of the disciples—Peter, James, and John—got to see this truth vividly realized, high on Mount Tabor, when Moses and Elijah suddenly appeared and conversed with Jesus (see Mark 9:2–8).

With Jesus the kingdom had indeed come in power, and its saintly subjects already enjoyed the privileges of citizenship. This was a fundamental part of the Christian faith from the beginning. The Letter to the Hebrews includes a long list of the faithful departed, encouraging us by their example. But the point is that they're not *really* departed:

And what more shall I say? For time would fail me to tell of Gideon, Barak, Samson, Jephthah, of David and Samuel and the prophets—who through faith conquered kingdoms, enforced justice, received promises, stopped the mouths of lions, quenched raging fire, escaped the edge of the sword, won strength out of weakness, became mighty in war, put foreign armies to flight. Women received their dead by resurrection. Some were tortured, refusing to accept release, that they might rise again to a better life. Others suffered mocking and scourging, and even chains and imprisonment. They were stoned, they were sawn in two, they were killed with the sword; they went about in skins of sheep and goats, destitute, afflicted, ill-treated—of whom the world was not worthy—wandering over deserts and mountains, and in dens and caves of the earth.

And all these, though well attested by their faith, did not receive what was promised, since God had foreseen something better for us, that apart from us they should not be made perfect.

Therefore, since we are surrounded by so great a cloud of witnesses, let us also lay aside every weight, and sin which clings so closely, and let us run with perseverance the race that is set before us, looking to Jesus the pioneer and perfecter of our faith, who for the joy that was set before him endured the cross, despising the shame, and is seated at the right hand of the throne of God. (Hebrews 11:32—12:2)

These heroes of old are a *cloud of witnesses* surrounding us. The writer assumes here what the Catholic Church has always taught: that the saints are still with us and still interested in our humble affairs. Wherever we go we have the company of people whose lives showed the truth of God's Word. Christians who died in the faith became part of that illustrious company.

Popular Devotions

Devotion to the saints was a normal expression of basic Christian faith—faith in the immortality of the soul and in the saving justice and mercy of God. Believing what they believed, and what we still believe today, Christians sought the help of the saints in heaven as confidently as they had sought their prayers when those saints had walked the earth. For faithful people, after all, "life is changed, not ended," at bodily death. "When the body of our earthly dwelling lies in death, we gain an everlasting dwelling place in heaven."[1]

Certain saints, predictably, attracted the ardent piety of a number of Christians. We find abundant evidence for early devotion to the apostles and to the Blessed Virgin Mary. A scrap of papyrus discovered in Egypt preserves the earliest instance of a Marian prayer that's still used today: "We fly to your patronage, O holy Mother of God; despise not our petitions in our necessities, but deliver us always from all dangers, O glorious and blessed Virgin. Amen." By the mid-200s that prayer was established well enough to be incorporated into the Egyptian Church's liturgy.

The Church's love for the Blessed Virgin, then as now, had its grassroots and its "official" expressions. Her image is painted on the walls of the Roman catacombs and engraved on cemetery markers in the Fayoum, in Egypt. She is depicted on common household items, such as oil lamps; and she figures prominently in much of the imaginative literature of the early Church—the spurious books known as New Testament apocrypha.

From around AD 250 comes our oldest surviving report of a Marian apparition. To St. Gregory the Wonderworker, the pioneering bishop of Armenia, she appeared, accompanied by St. John the apostle. Christians kept the memory of that event, and a little over a century later it was set down in detail by another Gregory, St. Gregory of Nyssa.

The early centuries were times of intense persecution, and so the martyrs were especially revered. The dates of their passing were carefully recorded, and Mass was offered in each martyr's memory on his or her *dies natalis*, or "birthday"—the day of passage to eternal life. So plentiful were these observances that Church calendars, with their brief biographies of the saints, came to be known as *martyrologies*.

The cult of a particular saint had its own character, partly conferred by God's grace, partly colored by Christians' response to that grace. The case of two early martyrs will illustrate how devotion could develop over time.

Sts. Perpetua and Felicity were young women living in Carthage, North Africa, as the second century turned to the third. They converted just as the emperor Septimius Severus enacted a law forbidding conversion to Christianity. (The law left "cradle Catholics" alone but targeted catechumens.) And so, in AD 203, Perpetua, a newlywed noblewoman, and Felicity, a slave, were arrested and condemned to death.

While imprisoned Perpetua kept a diary in which she recorded her hopes and fears, her feelings for her family, and her experiences in prayer. When she died in the arena, the Christians of Carthage copied her journal and sent it abroad. Soon it was world-famous. Scenes from her narrative turn up in early Christian artwork in Europe.

The names of Perpetua and Felicity were on Christian lips throughout the empire. Soon they found a permanent place in the Eucharistic Prayer of the Roman liturgy—where they remain today. Thus two young women living far from the nerve centers of the world were able to gain lasting renown and devotion because they died for Christ.

Or consider St. Menas. Ancient accounts say he succumbed during the persecution of the emperor Diocletian, at the end of the third century. A soldier in the Roman army, he was exposed as a Christian and beheaded for his faith. His comrades then bore his body back home to Egypt. According to legend the camels stopped at a certain point and refused to go on. And there Menas was laid to rest.

Soon pilgrims appeared, churches sprang up, and a veritable city arose around the burial place of St. Menas. Situated near the Nile delta, the shrine—sometimes called the "Lourdes of the Ancient World"—flourished as a destination for pilgrims. People traveled there to bathe in its healing waters and to fill flasks to carry home for ailing friends and family members. Soon after the empire became officially Christian, Emperor Arcadius had a basilica built at the site.

The pilgrim flasks still turn up throughout the Middle East and even as far away as Spain and France. Mass-produced as souvenirs, they usually show the saint between two camels—representing the camels that sited his shrine. Around the image you'll usually find inscribed in Coptic or Greek, "Blessings of St. Menas."

The reverence first given to apostles and martyrs was eventually extended to the greatest of the desert solitaries, to exemplary bishops, and to those who performed extraordinary deeds of charity.

The Power of Dust and Ashes

Christians kept the feasts of the martyrs. They built shrines honoring them. They recorded their trials and last words with great care, purchasing court transcripts from the pagan authorities and attending the gruesome executions. These early Christian reports, called "acts of the martyrs," were models for the later "lives of the saints." Like Perpetua's diary, they were copied and circulated widely.

Another way of honoring the martyrs was to bury their bodies properly. The Christians had to put a lot of effort into collecting these relics—whatever bone or blood or ash was left after the pagans had finished their sport with the body. Roman authorities knew that Christians venerated martyrs and were not always willing to hand over a corpse that might become yet another illegal cult object.

Christians would build altars and places of worship above or near the burial place of someone who was recognized as a saint. The ancient churches of Rome bear testimony to this fact. Their altars may stand high on a dais, but archeologists know that excavating directly underneath the altars will reveal the tombs of the saints. This is how the bones of Sts. Peter and Paul were discovered.

While the souls of the just reside beneath heaven's altar (see Revelation 6:9), their *relics* rest beneath Christian altars on earth. Said St. Paulinus of Nola, a friend of St. Augustine and St. Ambrose: "Under the lighted altar, a royal slab of purple marble covers the bones of holy men. Here God's grace sets before you the power of the apostles by the great pledges contained in this meager dust."[2]

The bones of the saints, like the bones of Elisha in the Old Testament (see 2 Kings 13:20–21), were known to work miracles. While a young student, St. Jerome used to while away his Sundays in the Roman catacombs, walking and praying amid the exposed remains of the martyrs. When he was an older man and a Scripture scholar, he wrote a broadside against a man, Vigilantius, who dared raise doubts about the veneration of relics.

> You say that the souls of Apostles and martyrs have their abode either in the bosom of Abraham, or in the place of refreshment, or under the altar of God, and that they cannot leave their own tombs, and be present where they will.... Will you lay down the law for God? Will you put the Apostles into chains? So that to the day of judgment they are to be kept in confinement, and are not with their Lord—even though it is written of them, "They

follow the Lamb wherever he goes" (Revelation 14:4). If the Lamb is present everywhere, the same must be believed respecting those who are with the Lamb.[3]

The Pagan Response

All this trafficking in bones and blood was repulsive to the pagan Romans, whose understanding of death was different from that of Christians, to say the least. To put it starkly, death was at best an uncertainty for pagans, at worst the beginning of a time of torment.

For a Christian, death was the gateway to eternal life. Christians looked forward to a bodily resurrection. More than that, because God had consented to become human, the body itself was sacred.

In spite of some of their philosophers' attempts to convince the pagans that death couldn't really be all that bad, it was a terrifying unknown. Corpses were filthy, unclean horrors. Seeing one, or even seeing a coffin, was an evil omen that could ruin the day. When processions of martyrs came through the streets, Christians cheered, and pagans turned away.

So we can imagine what pagans must have thought about Christians who worshiped their strange God among the tombs of the martyrs. And we don't have to imagine it, because the pagans were not silent on the subject. They eagerly expressed the visceral horror they felt at the very idea of spending time in the company of corpses. And perhaps the most eloquent among them was the last pagan emperor, Julian.

Julian was one of the most formidable opponents Christian thinkers had ever faced. Unlike other pagan thinkers who had taken it upon themselves to dispute with Christians, Julian knew Christianity from the inside. He had been raised a Christian and was even well educated in the faith. He had paid attention. If someone quoted Scripture at him, he could quote it right back.

But Julian fell under the influence of pagan teachers and passionately repudiated his Christian faith—earning him the title "Julian the Apostate" in Christian literature. (Note that his family, nominal Christians though they were, had been a bunch of backstabbing hypocrites. If that was Christianity, no wonder Julian turned his back on it.) He combined a nostalgia for the good old days of Roman paganism with a Christian-style missionary zeal.

In spite of his Christian upbringing, Julian's sensibilities were thoroughly pagan when it came to dead bodies. So it's no surprise that he used the cult of dead bodies as one of his sticks with which to beat the Christians.

> Meanwhile, you keep adding more dead bodies on top of the corpse from long ago. You have filled up the world with tombs and cemeteries. But nowhere do your scriptures tell you to cower among the tombs and honor them.
>
> You have fallen so far into evil that you think you need not even hear the words of Jesus of Nazareth on this subject: "Woe to you, scribes and Pharisees, hypocrites! for you are like whitewashed tombs, which outwardly appear beautiful, but within they are full of dead men's bones and all uncleanness" [Matthew 23:27]. Now, if Jesus told you that tombs are "full of all uncleanness," how can you pray to God there?
>
> So why *do* you creep among the tombs? Would you like to know why? Not I, but the prophet Isaiah, will tell you: you "sit in tombs, and spend the night in secret places" [Isaiah 65:4] to have visions in dreams.
>
> You see how long ago the Jews practiced this sorcery, sleeping among tombs to have visions in dreams. And your apostles probably did the same, after their teacher died, and passed it on to you from the beginning—meaning to those who first took up

your religion. They cast their spells with more skill than you do, and openly showed off the places where they performed this sorcery and abomination.[4]

This is less an argument than an insult. Julian probably knew that the Christians weren't practicing sorcery in the tombs of the martyrs. But he also knew that the Christians had a deep-seated horror of witchcraft and sorcery, which they regarded as dealings with the devil, and he aimed right for the jugular. Take that, you filthy tomb-huggers!

Julian imagined a world where his own success in restoring and expanding the empire would bring most people back into the pagan fold. Three years into his reign, he set out with the extraordinarily ambitious goal of conquering the Persian Empire and making it a Roman province—but he was killed in battle. His last words, tradition reports, were, "You win, Galilean."[5]

That was the last gasp of official paganism in Rome. At Julian's funeral the pagan Libanius lamented that the Christians had come roaring back with a vengeance. The future of paganism had looked so rosy with Julian in charge:

> And here we were thinking that…the grave-houses would be replaced by temples, and everyone would be willing to come up to the altars; and that those who before had overturned them would themselves be setting them up; and that those who before had kept away from the blood of the victims would be offering sacrifices of their own free will.[6]

Instead Julian's new temple construction projects were immediately stopped, leaving great hulking skeletons of unfinished buildings for the Christians to laugh at. Pagan priests who had received hefty donations from the emperor were forced to pay them back—which, Libanius says, often ruined the priests or, worse, landed them in prison if they couldn't pay. The age of temples was over; the grave-houses—churches built on the tombs of the martyrs—had won.

In fact, there grew a Christian legend that Julian had been killed not by a Persian spear but by the direct intervention of a Christian saint. Imprisoned by Julian before the Persian campaign, St. Basil (who had grown up with Julian) prayed to St. Mercurius, a soldier and martyr, for help. St. Mercurius appeared to him and told him that he had killed Julian with a spear.[7] In some Eastern churches you can find icons of St. Mercurius thrusting a spear through the fallen emperor. It would be hard to think of a more appropriate symbolism: The cult of the saints had mortally wounded paganism.

CHAPTER FIVE

Purgatory: Love Stronger Than Death

On Sunday we pick up the parish bulletin and glance through the list of the week's Masses. Among the intentions we see names we recognize—old friends who have passed on, parishioners we have heard of but never knew, relatives of neighbors. Votive Masses for the dead are part of the Catholic landscape, like candles and stained glass.

Prayer for the dead has been a fixture of Christian devotion in every age. We believe that a bond of charity unites us even with those who have passed from earthly life. We have already seen how the saints in heaven exercise their charity for us on earth. In this chapter we'll see how the earthly Church, in its earliest years, practiced charity toward Christians who died unprepared for heaven. For "nothing unclean shall enter [heaven]" (Revelation 21:27).

Purgatory is an intermediate state of purification after death. Souls whose ultimate destination is heaven but who have died without repenting of some minor sins, or have not finished making satisfaction for the sins of which they have repented, must be purified before they can enter heaven and be with God for eternity. St. Paul tells us that our works will be measured, and what is worthless will be refined out of us.

> Now if any one builds on the foundation [Christ] with gold, silver, precious stones, wood, hay, straw—each man's work will become manifest; for the Day will disclose it, because it will be revealed with fire, and the fire will test what sort of work each one has done. If the work which any man has built on the foundation survives, he will receive a reward. If any man's work is burned up, he will suffer loss, though he himself will be saved, but only as through fire. (1 Corinthians 3:12–15)

The idea of praying for the dead was not new with Christianity. We read in the second book of Maccabees that the Jews believed that their prayers could deliver the dead from their sins.

After a bloody battle Judas Maccabeus discovered that the men who had died were wearing good-luck charms from pagan idols. (Obviously the charms weren't as lucky as they were advertised to be. Indeed, "it became clear to all that this was why these men had fallen" [2 Maccabees 12:40].) But the men had died fighting for Israel, so Judas led the people in praying that they might be forgiven for their idolatry.

> So they all blessed the ways of the Lord, the righteous Judge, who reveals the things that are hidden; and they turned to prayer, begging that the sin which had been committed might be wholly blotted out. And the noble Judas exhorted the people to keep themselves free from sin, for they had seen with their own eyes what had happened because of the sin of those who had fallen. He also took up a collection, man by man, to the amount of two thousand drachmas of silver, and sent it to Jerusalem to provide for a sin offering. In doing this he acted very well and honorably, taking account of the resurrection. For if he were not expecting that those who had fallen would rise again, it would have been superfluous and foolish to pray for the dead. But if he was look-

ing to the splendid reward that is laid up for those who fall asleep in godliness, it was a holy and pious thought. Therefore he made atonement for the dead, that they might be delivered from their sin. (2 Maccabees 12:41–45)

So before the time of Christ, at least some Jews believed in an intermediate state after death that could be affected by prayer. Indeed, orthodox Jews still believe in a purification after death, and they pray for the repose of the departed.

A Teaching of Tradition

There is no direct mention of purgatory in Scripture—as indeed there is no direct mention of many other Christian doctrines (like the Trinity, for example). The teaching is implied by what we read in Paul and Maccabees and elsewhere in Scripture: If we pray for the dead, we must believe they are still in some state in which our prayers can affect them. But the belief is only implicit in Scripture; the tradition of the Church makes it explicit.

Tertullian warns Christians against demanding that every Christian belief be found explicitly in Scripture.

> You say that we must demand written authority even when we plead tradition. So then, let us ask whether tradition should not be admitted unless it is written. Certainly we must say that it should not be admitted, if we can find no precedent in any other practices that we keep up on the basis of tradition alone and the sanction of custom, without any written documentation."[1]

Tertullian goes on to mention practices he considers to be indisputably Christian: baptism in water according to a certain form, the celebration of the Eucharist, making the Sign of the Cross. And he mentions, "Whenever an anniversary comes around, we make offerings for the dead as birthday honors."

Though Tertullian admits that offerings for the dead are made only on the authority of Tradition, the custom must be a very ancient one, because Tertullian himself is very ancient—he was writing a little after the year 200—and the tradition was old in his time. Christians pray for the dead because the dead can benefit from their prayers—the dead who are in purgatory, that is.

At any rate, by the time of Origen, the doctrine of purgatory was well known in Catholic theology:

> For if you have built on the foundation of Christ not just gold, silver, and precious stones, but also wood, hay, and stubble, then what do you expect when your soul leaves your body?
>
> Do you think you would go into heaven, with your wood and hay and stubble, and defile the kingdom of God that way?
>
> Or do you think that you would be kept out and have no reward for your gold and silver and precious stones? That wouldn't be fair either.
>
> So what's left is that you will be sent to the fire that will burn off the worthless matter. For people who understand heavenly things call our God a cleansing fire. But this fire does not burn up the person, but only what the person himself has built— wood, hay, and stubble. It is obvious that the fire destroys the wood of our sins, and then returns to us the reward of our great works.[2]

Ripped From Our Impurity

St. Gregory of Nyssa recalled a conversation he had with his sister, St. Macrina, after the death of their brother, St. Basil. (They were an extraordinary family of saints, whose grandmother had been a martyr.) Gregory had been overcome by grief and doubt at the loss of his beloved brother, but Macrina gently led him back to certainty.

When they came to the subject of purgatory, Macrina—whom Gregory calls "the Teacher"—explained that the torments of purgatory are not so much a punishment as simply an inevitable consequence of an impure soul's being drawn out of its impurity.

So if the soul is not weighed down with extraneous things, and no trouble with the body is holding it down, its progress toward the One who pulls it up is pleasant and easy.

But suppose that it has been held in place by the nails of longing for earthly things—like a body crushed in the mound of rubble left by an earthquake. Imagine bodies not just held down by the ruins, but pierced through with spikes and splinters of rubble. What would naturally happen to those bodies when they were dragged from the wreckage by relatives to be given holy burial? Wouldn't they be all mangled and torn, disfigured in the most horrible manner you can imagine, with the nails under the pile tearing them by the sheer force needed to pull them out?

I think the situation of the soul is like that when the divine force, precisely because of God's love for man, drags what belongs to God from the wreckage of the irrational and the material. I don't think God brings all this pain on sinners out of hatred or revenge for a wicked life. He is only claiming and bringing back to him what he brought into existence at his own pleasure. But while he, for the very best reasons, is pulling the soul toward himself—toward the fountain of all blessedness— that very attraction must necessarily be a state of torture.

The refiners who separate the gold from the dross in it must melt, not only the base alloy, but also the gold itself; then, while the base metal is being consumed, the gold remains. In just the same way, while evil is being consumed in the fire of purgatory, the soul welded to that evil must inevitably be in the fire as well, until the base metal is all burned up and destroyed by the fire.[3]

The Voices of Ordinary Believers

The loudest witnesses for purgatory are not the theologians—important as they are—who wrote in exalted language for the consumption of other theologians. No, the loudest witnesses are the ordinary believers who scratched their humble inscriptions by the tombs of loved ones. "Everyone who understands these things, pray for me." "Remember to pray for…" "Pray for the soul of…"

Those early believers do not speak to the educated few: They speak to you and me as we walk through the catacombs today or even as we read about their inscriptions in a book. These were ordinary faithful believers who wanted to make sure that, as long as the catacombs were there—as long as faithful Christians visited the tombs of the departed saints—someone would be praying for the souls of their loved ones.

We can tease out whatever hints of doctrine we like from the best prose stylists of the day, but the graffiti in the catacombs tell us—with a loud, clear voice—what Christians universally believed.

Nor were passing Christians the only audience for these scratchy messages to eternity. A graffito near the tomb of St. Peter asks for the prayers of the saint himself for the other Christians buried nearby: "Peter, pray for the pious Christian men interred next to your body."[4]

Masses for the dead are one of the ways we make our prayers today, and we know that the tradition has a long history. We can find the idea presented unambiguously in one of the great literary masterpieces from the patristic era—the *Confessions* of St. Augustine.

St. Augustine remembered how, in his last days with his mother, Monica, at Ostia, she expressed her joy that he was finally brought into the Catholic faith. The hope that she would live to see that was the only reason she had for staying alive into old age. "Why am I still here?" she asked.

> But just five days later, or not much more, she came down with a fever. And while she was sick one day she fainted, and for a short time was unconscious of visible things. We rushed to her side, but she came back to her senses soon enough, and looking at my brother and me as we stood next to her, she asked us, "Where was I?"
>
> Then, looking straight at us as we stood there dumbstruck with grief, she said, "You will bury your mother here."
>
> I was silent, and held my tears back. But my brother said something about wishing—as if it were a better thing—that she could die in her own country and not abroad.
>
> When she heard that, she fixed him with an anxious stare, as if to stop him from thinking such things. Then she turned to me. "See what he's saying!" she said. And shortly after that she told both of us, "Lay this body anywhere, and don't trouble yourselves at all about how you care for it. This is all I ask: that you remember me at the Lord's altar wherever you may be."
>
> And when she had given us that opinion in what words she was able to speak, she fell silent. For she was in pain with her worsening disease.[5]

What St. Monica asked for is exactly what we see in our weekly bulletins today: to be remembered at Mass after she was gone. The long night of the Dark Ages had already begun to close in on the empire, but the tradition of Masses for the dead would endure. Indeed, that tradition has hardly changed in sixteen centuries or more.

CHAPTER SIX

The Clergy: Love's Earthly Form

Catholic clergy today have a difficult job. Their congregations expect them to be orators, teachers, CEOs, and psychologists—busy, bottom-line oriented, yet always available too. Meanwhile the media consistently portray them as hypocrites and villains.

But the priesthood has never been easy. Consider the case of just one little parish from the Church's first generation.

The church of Corinth was a lively community. Their city was a prosperous center of trade and culture. The people were accomplished and well educated. But they were also prideful, with a tendency toward self-justification and cliquishness. To say that some were confused about sexual morality would be an understatement. The Christians in Corinth had an unfortunate tendency to bring their problems with them to Mass—observing social divisions, neglecting the poor, and eating like gluttons.

St. Paul dedicated two long letters—a rather large share of the New Testament—to the task of bringing this Greek church to order. He corrected the personal faults of some individuals, but mostly he urged the Corinthians to greater unity and fidelity by means of more faithful worship. He focused on liturgy and sacraments and the respective roles of the Church's ministers and laypeople.

Eucharistic worship was St. Paul's key to a Church that is one, holy, catholic, and apostolic: "Because there is one bread, we who are many are one body, for we all partake of the one bread" (1 Corinthians 10:17).

Succeeding With Succession

If Paul achieved any success, it was short-lived. We know this because we have a letter written by the Church of Rome and addressed to the Church of Corinth, and it was probably sent off around AD 67. It bears the name of the one of the earliest popes, St. Clement of Rome.

It had been at least a decade since Paul wrote his letters. He had gone on to Rome, where he died a martyr's death in the persecution of the emperor Nero. In the years in Rome before his death, Paul had drawn many disciples to Christ, among them (quite likely) Clement. This man was among those who assumed the mantle of Peter and Paul and were left to continue the pastoral care of the Church's far-flung congregations.

And now word reached Rome that the Christians of Corinth had gone into rebellion and deposed their clergy. This sad situation drew a long letter of exhortation and discipline from Rome. Clement invokes the authority of the Holy Spirit as he calls for order in the church of Corinth. He notes that order—harmony—is the hallmark of everything God makes and gives. There is design in the cosmos, and we see it in the regular passage of the seasons and movement of the heavenly bodies. There was order in Israel's kingdom and Jerusalem's temple of the Old Testament. Likewise, when Jesus, the God-Man, established his Church, he gave it—and likewise its public worship—a certain harmonious form.

The apostles received the Gospel for us from the Lord Jesus Christ; Jesus Christ was sent forth from God. So Christ is from God, and the apostles are from Christ. Both therefore came of the will of God in the appointed order. Having received their orders… they went forth with the good news that the kingdom of God was to come. So preaching everywhere, in country and town, they appointed their first-fruits, when they had proved them by the Spirit, to be bishops and deacons to those who should believe.…

Our Apostles knew through our Lord Jesus Christ that there would be contention over the office of bishop. That is why, having received complete foreknowledge, they appointed the aforesaid persons, and afterward they gave the offices a permanent character, that if these should fall asleep, other approved men should succeed to their ministry.[1]

Thus Clement explained the idea that came to be known as "apostolic succession"—the Church's guarantor of perpetual continuity in ministry. This manifested itself most visibly, of course, in the Church's worship, in the Mass. There were no Catholic schools back then. The Church could not really own property. So the clergy's domain—as pastors, teachers, and rulers—was the liturgy, where they had leadership roles quite distinct from the role of the laity.

And where and by whom he would have [the rites] performed, he himself fixed by his supreme will: that all things should be done with piety according to his good pleasure and might be acceptable to his will.… For to the high priest his proper services have been assigned, and to the priests their proper office has been appointed, and upon the Levites their proper ministrations are laid. The layman is bound by the layman's ordinances. Let each of you, brethren, in his own order give thanks unto God, maintaining a good conscience and not transgressing the appointed liturgical norm, but acting appropriately.[2]

Imitating Angels

The integrity of the Church's hierarchy was a pressing concern of that first generation. Church order is a recurring theme in the letters of St. Ignatius and St. Polycarp of Smyrna. Writing around AD 107, Ignatius asserts that each local church has "one Eucharist, for there is one flesh of our Lord Jesus Christ, and one cup for union with his blood, one altar, as there is one bishop with the presbyters and the deacons."[3]

Thus we find at that early date the three orders of clergy that the Church still recognizes today: bishop, priest, and deacon. As with Clement just a few years before, Ignatius held that this arrangement should be harmonious, in accordance with God's will: "Be zealous to do all things in harmony with God, with the bishop presiding in the place of God, and the priests in the place of the council of the apostles, and the deacons, who are most dear to me, entrusted with the service of Jesus Christ."[4]

It is noteworthy that Ignatius treats the subject consistently as he deals with several different churches throughout the Roman world. It is noteworthy too that he does not *argue* for this three-level arrangement but rather *assumes* that it is already established and urges Christians to be faithful to the tradition. (St. Polycarp of Smyrna, Ignatius' contemporary, treats this arrangement the same way in his Letter to the Philippians.)

Documents of the third century say that the three-level hierarchy predates even the teaching of Jesus Christ and was simply the Church's adaptation of Israel's clerical hierarchy—with high priest,

priest, and Levite corresponding directly to the Church's bishop, priest, and deacon. In the first years of the third century, St. Clement of Alexandria, in Egypt, said the hierarchical order predated Israel as well—and even creation itself! "In the Church," he says, "there is a gradation of bishops, priests, and deacons, which is, I believe, an imitation of the glory of angels."[5] Thus the Church's hierarchy, according to Clement, is a reflection of the heavenly hierarchy.

The bishop was the ordinary celebrant of the Eucharist. He presided, as Ignatius said, in the place of God, and he held the fullness of priesthood. Every bishop was a presbyter, but only one presbyter was bishop in the local church. (*Presbyteros* is the Greek word for "elder" and the word from which we get the English *priest*.)

The bishop was the individual most clearly identified with his local church. In AD 255 St. Cyprian said: "The bishop is in the Church, and the Church is in the bishop, and if anyone is not with the bishop, he is not in the Church."[6] As the churches grew, however, it became necessary for bishops to delegate many of the everyday liturgical duties to their priests.

The offices and titles appear in the New Testament, with their duties spelled out especially in the pastoral epistles to Timothy and Titus. They are evident as well in the Acts of the Apostles. There we see the apostles calling men to ministry and then empowering them for ministry with a consistent ritual act: the laying on of hands (see Acts 6:6 and 13:2–3). This is the ritual we've come to know as ordination, the sacrament we know as "holy orders."

For Clement of Rome the offices had a permanent character: they were intended to last as long as the Church. But the priesthood of the man ordained also had a permanent character. St. Augustine taught that holy orders was, in this way, like baptism: "Each is a sacrament and is given by a certain consecration: the one when a man is baptized, the other when he is ordained, and so in the Catholic Church it is not permitted to repeat either."[7]

Only a bishop could validly ordain priests. Then as now, only men could be ordained. A fourth-century compilation, the Apostolic Constitutions, recognizes the work of women called "deaconesses" but emphasizes that they may not pronounce blessings or fulfill any function proper to a priest or deacon.

Priesthood was a tremendous gift, but it called men to a life of tremendous sacrifice. Some of the Roman persecutions targeted only the Christian clergy; and the clergy were always the easiest targets anyway, because they were often publicly identified with the Church. More was expected from men who were ordained because they had received extraordinary grace with the laying on of hands. They received power, authority, and a certain dignity, at least within the congregation. St. John Chrysostom said:

> The office of the priesthood is exercised on earth, but it ranks among things that are heavenly, and with good reason. For it was neither a man nor an angel nor an archangel nor any other created power, but the Paraclete himself who established this ministry.... If you consider what it is for a man clothed in flesh and blood to be able to approach that pure and blessed nature, you will easily understand to what a dignity the grace of the Holy Spirit has raised priests.[8]

A Manual for the Clergy

St. Ambrose, a bishop of Milan in the 300s, wrote a manual to help his clergy live up to the dignity of their office. His *On the Duties of the Clergy* is as relevant today as it was more than sixteen hundred years ago. Its three volumes give not only sound advice that any minister should follow but also a vivid picture of the Christian clergy in the days just after Christianity had finally displaced paganism in the Roman Empire.

The Case for Celibacy

The rule of celibacy was already in place in the Western Church by Ambrose's time, but he makes a careful distinction between that *rule* and what he regards as the immutable *law* that a priest can marry only once. "In some outlying areas" there were married priests with children, but Ambrose had to explain that fact to his audience of young priests in Milan, which by this time had surpassed Rome as the greatest city in the West. Ambrose assumed that the priests he was talking to had always been celibate; he explains that the law, however, is that no one who has been married *twice* can become a priest, and a married man who becomes a priest cannot marry again. In branches of the Catholic Church where married clergy are allowed, this is still the law today, as it is in Eastern Orthodox churches.

> But what shall I say about chastity, when only one marriage is allowed, and not a second?
>
> On marriage, the law is not to marry again or to look for union with a second wife.
>
> Many find it strange that a second marriage before baptism should be an impediment, preventing a man from being elected to the clerical office and receiving the gift of ordination. After all, even crimes don't usually stand in the way, once they've been wiped away in the sacrament of baptism.
>
> But we must remember that *sin* can be forgiven in baptism, but *law* cannot be abolished. In the case of marriage, there is no *sin*, but there is a *law*. Whatever sins you have can be wiped away,

but whatever law there is cannot be set aside in marriage. How could a man encourage [a widow to forsake remarriage] when he himself has been married more than once?

But you know that the office of minister must be kept pure and immaculate, and must not be defiled by sexual intercourse —you know this, as I say, if you have received the gifts of the sacred ministry, with pure bodies and unspoiled modesty, and without ever having enjoyed sexual intercourse. I mention this only because, in some outlying areas, when they enter the ministry, or even when they become priests, they have begotten children. They defend this on the ground of ancient custom—from the time when the sacrifice was offered at long intervals.

Even the people, however, had to purify themselves two or three days before, as we read in the Old Testament [see Exodus 19:10]. They even used to wash their clothes. If they were so careful in what was only the *figure,* how much more careful we ought to be with the *reality!*

So learn, priest and Levite, what it means to wash your clothes. You must have a pure body with which to offer the sacraments. If the people were forbidden to approach the sacrifice unless they washed their clothes, do you dare to make supplication for others while you are filthy in heart and body? Do you dare to make an offering for them?[9]

Beware of Ambition

In Ambrose's time the Church was no longer a persecuted minority: It was the favored religion of the empire, rapidly becoming the only really legal religion. Bishops were enormously powerful: Ambrose himself, as we saw in chapter two, forced the emperor Theodosius to his knees in public penance for atrocities he had committed after a revolt in Thessalonica. And the Church was open to anyone with talent: A Christian didn't have to be from one of the great families.

All those things conspired to make the Church very attractive to ambitious men looking for a career path rather than a true vocation. That's a danger that Ambrose had to fight, but carefully. There is a laudable ambition that sees rising in the Church as an opportunity to render more service, and there is a deplorable ambition that looks for power. Ambrose carefully advises his young priests that in the Church you get ahead by your virtue, not by your ruthless pursuit of promotion.

> So I think that we should work to gain preferment—especially in the Church—only by good actions, and for the right reasons. There should be no haughty pride, no idle carelessness, no shameful motives, no inappropriate ambition. A plain simplicity of mind is all you need, and it recommends itself quite sufficiently.
>
> When you're in office, you shouldn't be harsh and strict, or too lenient. We shouldn't look like tyrants on the one hand, or like lazy placeholders on the other.
>
> And we must work to win over many by the kindnesses and duties in our power, and to hold onto the good opinion people already have of us. People will forget the good we've done before—and with good reason—if they have a wrong to complain of now. For it often happens that someone we've shown favor to, letting him rise step by step, will be driven away if we put someone else in front of him in some unworthy way. But it is appropriate for a priest to show favor in his kindnesses and decisions in such a way that he is always fair, and to show the same regard for other clergy that he would for his own parents.

If you have had a good reputation, you shouldn't become over-bearing, but rather stand firm in your humility, bearing in mind the grace you have received. A priest shouldn't be offended if a cleric or attendant, or anyone else in the Church, should win praise by showing mercy, or by fasting, or by an upright life, or by teaching and reading. For the grace of the Church is the praise of the teacher. It's good that someone else's work should be praised, as long as it's done with no desire to boast. Everyone should be praised by the lips of his neighbor, and not by his own mouth. Everyone should be commended by the work he has done, not by what he wanted to do.

But if anyone disobeys his bishop, and wants to push himself up and overshadow his bishop's merits by putting on a false appearance of education, humility, or mercy, his pride is leading him away from the truth. For the rule of truth is to do nothing to advance yourself that actually makes you go backward, and not to use whatever good you have to disgrace or blame some-one else.[10]

As He Said, So He Did

There was no better example of Ambrose's advice in action than Ambrose himself. He wielded almost unbelievable power, but he did it only by his example, not because of his ambition. He never sought power; rather, it came to him because he showed he could be trusted with it better than anyone else. True, he forced Theodosius to his knees, but in fact there was no force involved. Ambrose made the emperor's sin clear to him, and Theodosius fell to his knees on his own.

Historians tell us that the Church was growing into a formidable power in the West at the time of Ambrose and that Ambrose himself helped it along a good bit. In the centuries to come, as the imperial power suddenly collapsed and Europe divided into myriad struggling barbarian kingdoms, the Church became the greatest power of all, the only force that could extend its reach right across the continent the way the old Roman Empire once had done.

Ambrose shows how this happened. By the time he disciplined Theodosius, he had already stared down two other emperors, Gratian and Valentinian—and perhaps more courageously, Valentinian's mother, Justina. He boiled the principle down to a phrase that could be, and maybe should be, engraved in stone: "The emperor is indeed with the Church, not above the Church."[11] For saying so Ambrose was prepared, he said, to suffer "the priest's usual fate."[12]

The Power of Holiness

The Church didn't conquer by arms: It conquered by outstanding virtue, exemplified quite often in its bishops and priests. The Church's greatest leaders were men like St. Ambrose, who defied emperors; St. Leo the Great, who went out to meet Attila the Hun armed with nothing but his virtue; and St. Gregory the Great, who led the people when they could find no other leaders. The power of the Church was in its ministers, and their power was not in any force they wielded but only in their holy example. They could not push the people in any direction; but they led, and the people willingly followed.

And nothing has really changed. Today the Church has no power to enforce its will. No one has to be Catholic; no one has to be Christian. The priests, deacons, and bishops who serve the Church have to persuade people that they *want* to be Christian, and the only way to do that is by an exceptionally holy life.

In return for that we, the ordinary believers, need to respect the hierarchical authority of the Church. That sometimes requires exercising active humility. It's easy to confuse our personal taste with objective truth—and that's why we have Church leadership in the first place. Our leaders are human, like us, all sinners and imperfect. But the leadership is a divine institution. It goes right back to Jesus Christ, in an unbroken line of apostles.

The Papacy:
The Apostolic Throne

These days, when the pope speaks people listen. If the pope sneezes the papers are full of speculations about his health. You can turn on the television and see the pope somewhere every day. A new encyclical is front-page news in *The New York Times*—hardly a Catholic-leaning paper. In a world of megacelebrities, the pope is the biggest celebrity of all.

It's an awful responsibility for the bishop of Rome, knowing that every single thing he says goes out almost instantly to a billion Christians. It goes out to even more non-Christians, because the world cares what the pope says. The world may not like it, but when the pope speaks about contraception, or economic justice, or even abstract ideas like whether there is absolute truth, the world listens, reacts, and debates.

Think how different it must have been in the time of the first pope. St. Peter was directly appointed by Christ, but who had ever heard of him? Only the few believers in the Way even knew who Peter was, and only the ones in Rome got to hear what he had to say. The Roman Empire was a big place, with no Internet or television, and Peter could only be in one city at a time. If believers were lucky, they might hear some news of Peter when a traveler returned from Rome. If they were very lucky, they might get a letter from Peter, which they would treasure as something more valuable than gold.

Even Peter's martyrdom probably didn't make the nightly news in Rome. Nero was executing so many people at the time that the gossip would have centered on which aristocrats were next to go. No one outside the little community of believers would have mentioned Peter's execution, unless somebody momentarily paused at the tavern to say, "Hey, did you hear about that Jew who got crucified *upside down?*"

Throughout several centuries a pope could be martyred or speak on an important issue, and a Christian in a far corner of the empire might not hear about it for years. It was a different world back then. The papacy had to be quite different too, but it was also the same. It grew from seedling to sapling to great shady tree, and through all those stages it was the same plant.

"You Are Peter"

We date the office of pope from the time Christ chose Peter to lead his Church:

> He said to them, "But who do you say that I am?" Simon Peter replied, "You are the Christ, the Son of the living God." And Jesus answered him, "Blessed are you, Simon Bar-Jona! For flesh and blood has not revealed this to you, but my Father who is in heaven. And I tell you, you are Peter, and on this rock I will build my Church, and the gates of Hades shall not prevail against it. I will give you the keys of the kingdom of heaven, and whatever you bind on earth shall be bound in heaven, and whatever you loose on earth shall be loosed in heaven." (Matthew 16:15–19)

The "keys of the kingdom" were symbolic authority; the person who held the keys was the king's prime minister, so to speak. When Isaiah delivered God's message that the wicked minister Shebna would be deposed and Eliakim given his place, he used almost the same words:

> In that day I will call my servant Eliakim the son of Hilkiah, and I will clothe him with your robe, and will bind your belt on him, and will commit your authority to his hand; and he shall be a father to the inhabitants of Jerusalem and to the house of Judah. And I will place on his shoulder the key of the house of David; he shall open, and none shall shut; and he shall shut, and none shall open. (Isaiah 22:20–22)

To anyone who knew Scripture, then, it was obvious that Christ was making Peter his first minister—an office we see him actually holding as soon as Christ ascended into heaven. Peter led the apostles in deciding to replace Judas; Peter spoke for all of them to the crowds at Pentecost; Peter made the final decision on admitting uncircumcised gentiles to the Church.

That doesn't mean Peter was always right about everything. Paul didn't hesitate to reprimand when he thought Peter's actions had not lived up to his own teaching.

> But when Cephas came to Antioch I opposed him to his face, because he stood condemned. For before certain men came from James, he ate with the Gentiles; but when they came he drew back and separated himself, fearing the circumcision party. And with him the rest of the Jews acted insincerely, so that even Barnabas was carried away by their insincerity. But when I saw that they were not straightforward about the truth of the gospel, I said to Cephas before them all, "If you, though a Jew, live like

a Gentile and not like a Jew, how can you compel the Gentiles to live like Jews?" (Galatians 2:11–14)

Cephas, of course, is *Peter* in Aramaic, the language Peter and Paul spoke at home. The point is not that Peter was always right but that he had authority. In the end it was Peter who decided that Paul was right: gentiles should be admitted to the Church without circumcision. At the Council of Jerusalem, Paul had his say, and the circumcision party had their say. Then Peter spoke, and it was decided. "Now therefore why do you make trial of God by putting a yoke upon the neck of the disciples which neither our fathers nor we have been able to bear? But we believe that we shall be saved through the grace of the Lord Jesus, just as they will" (Acts 15:10–11).

No matter how many converts Paul made, no matter how many letters he wrote, he never had the authority to decide a matter finally for the whole Church the way Peter did. He could and did argue with Peter, but Paul got his way only because Peter was persuaded.

Appealing to Rome

Before Peter died he appointed a successor—St. Linus. His successor as bishop of Rome—the capital of the known world—inherited his position as leader of the Church, the pope. We can see from the start an obvious deference to Rome, an assumption that the bishop of Rome had the right to intervene in the affairs of other churches and decide disputes when they came up.

Clement, another one of the early popes, wrote the letter we have already seen, disciplining the congregation in Corinth. What's notable is that Clement acknowledges from the start that he is writing in response to an appeal from that distant church. He assumes that he has the authority to reply in an authoritative way and that they will recognize his authority.

> Because a number of sudden disasters have happened to us one after another, we fear that we are a little late in addressing the questions you asked us. We especially need to address that shameful and repulsive sedition, completely abhorrent to God's chosen, which a few foolish and self-confident people have whipped up to such a frenzy that your honorable and illustrious name, worthy to be universally loved, has been badly tarnished.[1]

The Corinthians, you'll remember, had tossed out some of their leaders for what Clement thought was no good reason. He told them that the office of bishop is a divine institution, and it can't be taken away arbitrarily at the whim of the congregation. Clement found such "sedition" repulsive, and his instructions are clear. The people who started it need to repent. If they act with humility, they can be welcomed back into the flock.

> Those of you who laid the foundation of this sedition, submit yourselves to the priests, and receive correction so as to repent, bending the knees of your hearts. Learn to submit, putting aside the proud and arrogant self-assurance of your tongue. For it is better for you to have a humble but honorable place in the flock of Christ, than to be highly exalted but cast out from the hope of his people....
>
> Send our messengers Claudius Ephebus and Valerius Bito, along with Fortunatus, back to us quickly and joyfully, that they may all the sooner bring us news that you have returned to the peace and harmony we so earnestly desire and long for, and that we may all the more quickly rejoice that you have put things back in good order. The grace of our Lord Jesus Christ be with you, and with all everywhere that are the called of God through him, by whom be to him glory, honor, power, majesty, and eternal dominion, from everlasting to everlasting. Amen.[2]

In closing the letter Clement speaks of his own authority in a way that would be considered arrogant if it were not true: "render obedience unto the things written by us through the Holy Spirit,"[3] and "if certain persons should be disobedient unto the words spoken by [Christ] through us, let them understand that they will entangle themselves in no slight transgression and danger."[4]

But Clement's authority was not considered arrogant. His ruling was welcomed in Corinth, and his fatherly letter was still read in the liturgy there more than a hundred years later. In some parts of the Church, it was considered part of the canon of the New Testament!

Ignatius's Deference to Rome

We can see the respect paid to Rome just a few years later by St. Ignatius of Antioch. On his way to trial and almost certain death in Rome, Ignatius wrote an encouraging letter to the Romans. Just as Clement assumed the honor and authority of his own position, we can see that Ignatius acknowledges the special position of Rome in the Church. Look how he greets the church in Rome:

> Ignatius, who is also called Theophorus,
> to the Church which has obtained mercy, through the majesty of the Most High Father, and Jesus Christ, his only-begotten Son;
> the Church which is beloved and enlightened by the will of him that wills all things which are according to the love of Jesus Christ our God,
> which also presides in the place of the region of the Romans, worthy of God, worthy of honor, worthy of the highest happiness, worthy of praise, worthy of obtaining her every desire, worthy of being deemed holy,
> and which presides over love, is named from Christ, and from the Father,

which I also salute in the name of Jesus Christ, the Son of the
Father:

to those who are united, both according to the flesh and spirit,
to every one of His commandments;

who are filled inseparably with the grace of God, and are purified from every strange taint:

Abundance of happiness unblameably, in Jesus Christ our God.[5]

Was Ignatius always so florid? No. We can compare the greeting in
one of his other letters, this one to the church in Magnesia:

Ignatius, who is also called Theophorus,

to the [Church] blessed in the grace of God the Father, in Jesus
Christ our Savior,

in whom I salute the Church which is at Magnesia, near the
Mæander,

and wish it abundance of happiness in God the Father, and in
Jesus Christ.[6]

The formula is the same: Ignatius identifies himself, identifies the
recipients, compliments the recipients, and wishes them all happiness in Christ. The difference is in the compliments. No other
church to which Ignatius wrote received a laundry list of compliments like the ones he gave Rome. It's obvious that Ignatius considers the Roman church supremely important.

That's especially significant because Ignatius had pretty strong
claims to be important himself. He was bishop of Antioch, where
Peter had been bishop before he moved to Rome. He was on his way
to martyrdom, himself an object of pilgrimage for Christians in
every city where his captors stopped along the way. He wrote letters
of instruction to the churches in all those places. If anyone on earth

had credentials as good as the bishop of Rome's, it would be Ignatius. Yet Ignatius defers to Rome.

The Line From Peter

Ignatius and Clement had known the apostles and had received their instructions from them directly. In the generations to come, we see that the deference to Rome continued.

When St. Irenaeus of Lyons was writing in the late 100s, there were already many heretical movements challenging the orthodox Church. A methodical and clear thinker, Irenaeus wrote a kind of encyclopedia of heresies, including both their major tenets and where they went wrong.

Irenaeus attacked the heretics with an unanswerable argument. Orthodox doctrine comes down from the apostles, who were taught by Christ; your heretical doctrines don't. He doesn't have space to show the successions of all the bishops, he says. But he'll show us the most important one: the tradition of the Church of Rome.

> In a book like this, it would be very dull to run through the successions of all the churches. But we can rout all those who, whether through selfishness, or vanity, or blindness and contrariness, or anything else, hold unauthorized meetings, just by showing the tradition of that greatest, most ancient, and universally known church founded and organized at Rome by the two most glorious apostles, Peter and Paul. The faith that church preaches comes down to us through successions of the bishops. For every church must necessarily look to this church because of its more powerful authority, through which the apostolic tradition has been preserved continuously by the faithful everywhere.
>
> When the blessed apostles had founded and built up this church, they appointed Linus as bishop. (Paul mentions this

same Linus in the Epistles to Timothy.)

Anacletus succeeded Linus.

After him, third place from the apostles, Clement was made bishop. Clement had seen and talked with the blessed apostles, so that you could say their preaching was still echoing in his ears, and their traditions were still before his eyes.[7]

Here Irenaeus summarizes Clement's letter to the Corinthians, pointing out that Clement spoke with the authority of the apostles. He continues:

Anyone who likes may see from this letter that God, the Father of our Lord Jesus Christ, was preached by the churches, and may understand the apostolic tradition of the Church, since this letter is older than these men who are now spreading falsehood, and who conjure into existence another god beyond the Creator and the Maker of all existing things.

After Clement came Evaristus.

Alexander came after Evaristus.

Then, sixth from the apostles, Sixtus was appointed.

After him came Telephorus, who was gloriously martyred.

Then came Hyginus;

after him, Pius;

then after him, Anicetus.

Sorer succeeded Anicetus.

Finally, after Sorer, Eleutherius has inherited the office of bishop, the twelfth from the apostles.

This is the order and succession by which the tradition of the church and the preaching of the truth have come down to us from the apostles. And this is all the proof we need that there is only one life-giving faith, which has been preserved in the

Church from the apostles down to our own time, and handed
down correctly.[8]

There are minor differences between Irenaeus's list and other lists,
but he makes his point precisely because everyone acknowledged
that there *was* a list. (In fact, we know of at least one list older than
that of Irenaeus, though we have no surviving copy.) It was a well-
known fact that you could trace the succession of the bishops of
Rome right back to St. Peter.

Communion With Rome

The Church historian Eusebius, who also gives us a succession list
for the bishops of Rome, records a very interesting event. There had
been trouble in Antioch over Paul of Samosata, the bishop of
Antioch, who was accused both of heresy and of immorality.
According to the orthodox bishops, he declared that Jesus Christ
was not divine, and he traveled with a kind of harem of beautiful
young women. Meeting at a council, the bishops removed Paul as
bishop of Antioch and substituted an orthodox bishop of blameless
reputation. But Paul the heretic refused to turn over the church
building, and he had friends in Antioch powerful enough to back
him up.

> Since Paul was now out of the bishop's seat, not to mention the
> orthodox faith, Domnus, as we said, became the bishop of
> Antioch.
>
> But Paul refused to surrender the church building. So a peti-
> tion was made to Emperor Aurelian. He decided the question
> quite fairly: he ordered that the building should be handed over
> to whoever the bishops of Italy, and the bishop of Rome, should
> decide. And so this man was driven out of the Church in disgrace
> by the secular power.[9]

What's interesting is the standard Aurelian used to make his decision. He certainly wasn't a Christian: He was treating the Christians mildly for the moment, but later he would launch yet another persecution against them. But even an outsider could see that the Christian Church was not just a bunch of disconnected local institutions. To be a Christian you had to be in communion with the rest of the Church. And how could an outsider know which one of two competing bishops, each with his supporters, was really in communion with the rest of the Church? It was obvious even to a pagan emperor that it must be the one who's in communion with Rome.

Over the course of the early centuries, appeals went up to Rome from many of the other major churches: from Carthage, from Smyrna, from Alexandria, from Constantinople, from Cappadocian Caesarea. When Christians differed with one another over the day to celebrate Easter, they went to Rome with the question. When some churches began to rebaptize members who had fallen into serious sin, the neighboring bishops brought Rome in to correct the situation. Rome's record of doctrinal steadiness is remarkable when compared with every other see in the ancient world. We can see why St. Augustine was moved to say that when the Apostolic See has spoken, *causa finita est*—the matter is settled.[10]

In the mid–fourth century, the great champion of orthodoxy St. Athanasius of Alexandria mentioned among his credentials the approval of Pope Liberius, the man whose office, he said, is the "apostolic throne" and whose bishops are the "apostolic men."[11] Athanasius reports a speech in which Liberius, like Clement before him, presumes a great authority—an authority inherited from St. Peter and ultimate on earth yet at the same time unified with the councils and the Fathers:

How is it possible for me to [rule] against Athanasius? How can we condemn a man, whom not one council only, but a second assembled from all parts of the world, has fairly acquitted, and whom the Church of the Romans dismissed in peace? Who will approve of our conduct, if we reject in his absence a man whose presence among us we gladly welcomed, and admitted him to our Communion? This is no ecclesiastical canon; nor have we had transmitted to us any such tradition from the Fathers, who in their turn received from the great and blessed Apostle Peter.[12]

None of this evidence means that the exercise of the papacy was exactly the same in the early centuries as it is now. It grew and developed, like any living thing. But it's quite obvious that the bishop of Rome had a supreme authority in the Church, even when, by the world's standards, he was a poor nobody who didn't dare venture far from the catacombs.

Then as now there was an order to the Church—an order that (as Clement pointed out to the Corinthians) was divinely instituted. In his own diocese each bishop had authority. But when it was necessary to have a final decision for the whole Church, the bishops looked to Rome.

Communion with Rome was the mark of unity, the visible sign that the Church was truly Catholic. When you come right down to it, for all the visibility of the papacy, for all the pomp and spectacle, that's pretty much the way it works now.

Sex and the Sexes

Sex is the greatest thing there is, and marriage puts an end to it.

That seems to be what pagans think in every age. If you read the graffiti preserved in ancient Pompeii or the magazines on sale at the supermarket checkout, the message is the same. Images celebrate sex, implicitly or explicitly. Pitchmen hawk their wares with claims that this or that possession will yield sexual attractiveness. Society tells children that there's something weirdly abnormal about them if they aren't getting regular sex. And when someone finally gets married, his friends (or hers) throw a big pity party.

It's not surprising that many modern Americans think divorce is a natural result of marriage. Rome was a sexualized society, very much like ours, and one where divorce was probably as common as it is with us. Certainly the biographies of the upper crust—the emperors and their friends and families—are full of divorces and remarriages reflecting shifting political alliances.

Julius Caesar, for example, had three wives: The first died in childbirth, but he divorced the second when she became moderately inconvenient for his political career. Tiberius, who was emperor when Christ was crucified, had been forced to divorce his wife and marry Augustus's widowed daughter in order to cement his position in the imperial succession.

Against these backgrounds the teachings of the Catholic Church seem weirdly medieval—in tune neither with the old Roman world nor the Brave New World we live in.

A Higher Standard

Even the law of the Old Testament assumed that divorces would happen. If a man didn't like his wife, he could write a bill of divorce, and she was gone.

> When a man takes a wife and marries her, if then she finds no favor in his eyes because he has found some indecency in her, and he writes her a bill of divorce and puts it in her hand and sends her out of his house, and she departs out of his house, and if she goes and becomes another man's wife, and the latter husband dislikes her and writes her a bill of divorce and puts it in her hand and sends her out of his house, or if the latter husband dies, who took her to be his wife, then her former husband, who sent her away, may not take her again to be his wife, after she has been defiled; for that is an abomination before the LORD, and you shall not bring guilt upon the land which the LORD your God gives you for an inheritance. (Deuteronomy 24:1–4)

We should remember that Deuteronomy is the law that was given to Israel after two notorious lapses into idolatry—first with the golden calf while Moses was on Mount Sinai, and then with Baal at Peor (see Exodus 32; Numbers 25). In spite of all the miracles they had seen on their way out of Egypt, the Israelites were extraordinarily hard-hearted. And this is the reason Jesus gives for divorce under the old covenant.

Now, the Pharisees liked nothing better than to devise little tests to trip Jesus up when he was preaching. One of their tests was about this law. "Let's see if he remembers that bit about divorce in Deuteronomy," they said to themselves. So they put on their best poker faces and approached Jesus.

> And Pharisees came up to him and tested him by asking, "Is it lawful to divorce one's wife for any cause?" He answered, "Have you not read that he who made them from the beginning made them male and female, and said, 'For this reason a man shall leave his father and mother and be joined to his wife, and the two shall become one flesh'? So they are no longer two but one flesh. What therefore God has joined together, let not man put asunder." They said to him, "Why then did Moses command one to give a certificate of divorce, and to put her away?" He said to them, "For your hardness of heart Moses allowed you to divorce your wives, but from the beginning it was not so. And I say to you: whoever divorces his wife, except for unchastity, and marries another, commits adultery." (Matthew 19:3–9)

As he always did, Jesus held people to a higher standard than the Law. The Law allowed divorce—not because it was a good thing, Jesus said, but because the people were so sinful that it couldn't be prevented. Christians are expected to stick to the original intention of creation: that man and woman should become "one flesh," an inseparable unity.

Yet Paul talks to the Galatians as though Christ has brought freedom rather than more restrictions:

> Now before faith came, we were confined under the law, kept under restraint until faith should be revealed. So that the law was our custodian until Christ came, that we might be justified by faith. But now that faith has come, we are no longer under a

custodian; for in Christ Jesus you are all sons of God, through faith. For as many of you as were baptized into Christ have put on Christ. There is neither Jew nor Greek, there is neither slave nor free, there is neither male nor female; for you are all one in Christ Jesus. (Galatians 3:23–28)

We can see a hint of what made Christianity so revolutionary, and such a threat to Roman society, in that famous last verse: "There is neither Jew nor Greek, there is neither slave nor free, there is neither male nor female." Right in the Church's most sacred writings, we find a dangerous notion that cuts at the heart of a firm Roman belief.

Women as Property

In Roman society, and in ancient Israelite society as well, all the power belonged to the men. Women had no real rights; they passed from the complete control of their fathers to the complete control of their husbands.

Roman literature is full of fathers lamenting the wasted effort they've put into raising daughters.[1] To them, sons were useful because they continued the family name, but daughters only sucked up food and money. And then when a girl grew up (meaning when she was just reaching puberty), the family had to pay an enormous dowry to get someone to marry her.

It's hardly any wonder then that many girls never made it that far. The birth of a girl was a terrible disappointment to her father. And there was an easy solution to the problem: The baby could be thrown out. She would be "exposed"—left outside with the garbage to die. Then she wouldn't take up precious resources that the family could use to raise sons.

Even many Romans who succumbed to sentiment and kept their

girl children were eager to get rid of them as soon as possible. A girl might be married off at the age of thirteen or so through an alliance arranged by her father. She was her father's property, and he could dispose of her as he wished. Technically Roman law required that the woman consent to her marriage, but the law also allowed a father to kill his daughter if she didn't consent!

When a woman married she became her husband's property. It didn't matter whether she was happy about it; in fact, it was assumed that she wouldn't be. The historian Paul Veyne writes, "The wedding night took the form of a legal rape from which the woman emerged 'offended with her husband' (who, accustomed to using his slave women as he pleased, found it difficult to distinguish between raping a woman and taking the initiative in sexual relations)."[2]

At the end of the second century, St. Clement of Alexandria summarized the various pagan schools of thought about marriage:

> Plato put marriage among the outward goods: it provides for the continuation of our species, and passes down our traditions like a torch to our children's children.
>
> Democritus rejects marriage and having children, on the grounds of the many inconveniences that come up, and the distraction from more important things.
>
> Epicurus agrees, along with the rest of those who find their good in pleasure and the absence of pain.
>
> The Stoics believe that marriage and child-bearing are indifferent things.
>
> The Peripatetics believe that they are good things.
>
> To sum up, pursuing their teachings by argument, the philosophers make themselves slaves to pleasure. Some of them take up with concubines, some with mistresses, and most with young boys.[3]

All of these philosophers looked at marriage purely from the point of view of the man. Whether it was good for the woman wasn't something they worried about. And divorce could be practically a death sentence for the woman: With no way to earn a living and no one to take care of her, what could she do?

Daughters of God

Imagine what revolutionaries the Christians must have seemed to be. "There is neither male nor female!"

Yes, these Christians believed that a woman was just as much a child of God as a man was. They insisted on treating her as a *person,* someone who had fundamental rights and an immortal soul. And that turned everything upside down.

Christians know marriage as a sacred bond that requires the consent of both parties. St. Clement of Alexandria insisted that the girl had to be old enough to know what she was getting into: "We call it fornication, not just when there is fornication per se, but also when a girl is given in marriage too early—that is, when a girl who is not mature yet is given in marriage, either of her own free will or by her parents."[4]

The Christian view was attractive to many women. It's hardly surprising that Christianity made a lot of female converts in its early years. Widows were held in special esteem. There were many who, even if they were widowed at a young age, devoted themselves to the Church rather than to the search for a man.

St. John Chrysostom had a story to tell about that. His mother was one of those young widows, and by all accounts she was a very attractive woman. Yet she did not remarry, and she maintained a spotless reputation. In writing to console a young woman who had recently lost her husband, John tells her how much not only the

Christians but the pagans as well admire a widow who chooses not to remarry:

> I remember one time, when I was still a young man, the sophist who taught me—a man who was second to none in his reverence for the [pagan] gods—expressed his admiration for my mother in front of a large company. As he usually did, he had been asking the people sitting next to him who I was. Someone said that I was the son of a widow, so he asked me how old my mother was and how long she had been a widow.
>
> I told him that she was forty years old, and it had been twenty years since she lost my father.
>
> He was astonished, and he turned to the rest of the company. "Heavens!" he cried in a loud voice, "what women those Christians have!"
>
> That's how much widowhood is admired and praised, not just by us, but even by people outside the Church.[5]

Christian marriage is a partnership rather than an ownership. The woman has to love the man as sincerely as he loves her. Both the man and the woman have to be suited for marriage, and they have to be in the right circumstances to raise a family.

"Not every man should take a wife," Clement advises, "nor should a man take just any woman. Only a man who is in the right circumstances should marry, and only the right woman at the right time, and for the sake of children. He should marry someone who is like him in every way, and who is not forced or compelled to love him."[6]

Pleasure and Purpose
It's not surprising that many pagans concluded that marriage was only a civic duty. A man married to give his children a pedigree. He might be much more interested in his prostitutes or young boys.

Pedophilia was considered quite normal in the upper circles of Roman society. The hero (or antihero) and narrator of Petronius's *Satyricon,* a rambling picaresque novel that satirizes the Roman aristocracy in the time of Nero, tells of nearly fighting a duel over the affections of a young boy named Giton. Only the intervention of the boy himself keeps his two suitors from killing each other.

> So we put our swords away, and Ascyltos said, "I'll put an end to our disagreement. Let the boy himself pick the man he likes. He should have the freedom to choose his friend."
>
> Now, I expected that, since we had known each other so long, I would have made a strong impression on the boy. So I jumped at the offer, and put our argument in the hands of the little judge.
>
> As soon as he had my consent, Giton—not wanting to seem hesitant—leaped up and chose Ascyltos.
>
> I was thunderstruck. I fell on the bed, and I wouldn't have survived my loss if I hadn't been too jealous of my rival to kill myself.[7]

This could have been a scene in any classic European novel—except that, in most later eras, the object of the duel would have been a grown woman instead of a little boy. But it was almost expected of an upper-class Roman that he would keep a few boys around.

Trajan, widely praised as a model emperor, was equally praised by the historian Dio Cassius for his moderation in drinking and pederasty: "Trajan was well known for justice, bravery, and modest habits.… Of course I realize that he loved boys and wine. But if those things had ever prompted him to commit or allow any immoral or evil act, he would have been criticized for it. Instead, he drank all he wanted but stayed sober, and when he dallied with boys he didn't harm anyone."[8]

A *moderate* pedophile was such a refreshing change from overindulgent emperors like Nero, who kept squadrons of boys on the payroll, all surgically altered to his exact specifications. By any modern standard Nero was a very sick man. In imperial Rome he was just overindulgent.

In a way Petronius, with his wearisome chronicling of every vice the Romans of Nero's time could possibly think up, was making the Christians' argument for them. He drew a bitingly sharp portrait of a world in which everyone pursued pleasure after pleasure, and no one was having any fun. The endless pursuit of pleasure is no pleasure; it only wears people out.

St. Cyprian knew this. He was a convert to Christianity in the mid-200s. He had been a successful lawyer. He could look at his weary former peers and say:

> There is nothing so delightful to the faithful soul as the healthy feeling of untainted modesty. Having conquered pleasure—that is the greatest pleasure. There is no greater victory than the victory over your own lust. If you conquer an enemy, you have been stronger than someone else; but if you conquer your lust, you have been stronger than yourself.... Defeat lust, and you defeat sin. Defeat lust, and you prove that the curse of humanity lies flattened at your feet. Defeat lust, and you have peace forever. Defeat lust, and you gain back your liberty....
>
> In fact, we must say that adultery is not pleasure, but mutual contempt. It cannot be delightful, because it kills both the soul and modesty.[9]

One reason Roman attitudes seem so repulsive to us is that we have a very different idea about children—and that difference is largely a Christian one. Pagan Romans saw children as property. A father even had the right to demand capital punishment for a wayward child. But to a Christian a child is a person, and killing children—be they in the womb or outside the womb—is murder.

It's no wonder that Christians were accused of subverting Roman morality. The accusation was entirely true: Christians contradicted the basis of the Roman family. The family-values types were up in arms. Imagine saying that women and children are persons with rights! If the Romans didn't stop them, these Christians might undermine the whole empire.

The Mysteries of Marriage

In the last century or so, it has been fashionable for historians to portray the early Christians as somehow "anti-marriage" or "anti-sex." The Fathers would be baffled by such a charge, though they would surely recognize the sort of culture that produced it.[1]

The Fathers clearly saw the natural good of sex and marriage. More than this, however, they saw the supernatural good of the marital bond—and they held all natural goods to be subordinate to this. Tertullian, a married man of the second century, could wax rapturous in praise of conjugal life:

> How shall we ever find words suitable to describe the happiness
> of a marriage that the Church arranges, the Sacrifice confirms,
> and the blessing seals, which angels witness, and to which the
> Father gives his consent? For not even on earth do children
> marry rightly and lawfully without their fathers' permission.
> How beautiful, then, the marriage of two Christians, two who
> are one in hope, one in desire, one in discipline, one in service.[2]

As our own culture has lost sight of the supernatural, our historians often lose sight of distinctions that were important to the ancients, distinctions that made Christians different from pagans and made their life more pleasant.

One early Christian whose reputation has suffered much at the hands of secular historians is St. John Chrysostom; and nowhere is he so misunderstood as in his teaching about sex and marriage. If you search the World Wide Web using the terms "John Chrysostom" and "sex," you'll find a mess of conflicting statements.

Part of the problem is with the saint's interpreters, and part of it is with his own voluminous writings—some 700 sermons, 246 letters, plus biblical commentaries, moral discourses, and theological treatises. When a man publishes so many thousands of words, an industrious enemy can pull together enough strands to make a strong rope for his hanging. And on the subject of marriage, John made it easy for his enemies. Indeed, his paper trail is so ambiguous as to seem bipolar.

When libertines want to caricature Christian teaching, they inevitably quote Chrysostom. One anti-Christian Web site condemns him as the arch-villain among "the Fathers of the Dark Age," pronouncing him guilty of an "anti-sex, prudish, kill-joy morality." Another site produces this gem purportedly from one of John's homilies: "It does not profit a man to marry. For what is a woman but an enemy of friendship, an inescapable punishment, a necessary evil, a natural temptation, a domestic danger, delectable mischief, a fault in nature, painted with beautiful colors?"[3]

The sexologist Havelock Ellis judged John to be more than a little repressed. And even so great a historian as Peter Brown found Chrysostom's vision of sexuality to be "anxious" and "bleak."[4]

On the other hand, John is also the Father most invoked by those who wish to exalt the Christian vision of marriage. The Orthodox theologian Vigen Guroian speaks of "Chrysostom's virtually unique contribution" to a positive Christian understanding of family life. He quotes John's famous description of love-making: "How do they become one flesh?" John asks, and then he answers his own question. "As if she were gold receiving purest gold, the woman receives the man's seed with rich pleasure, and within her it is nourished, cherished, and refined. It is mingled with her own substance and she then returns it as a child!"[5]

Gold receiving gold—that doesn't sound like an "anti-sex, prudish, kill-joy morality."

So how do we reconcile these two sides of Chrysostom? Do we dismiss him as a hypocrite? Do we write him off as a hyper-clericalist who held married people to a lower moral standard than monks?

No. I believe both sets of quotations—the harangue and the poetry—make sense in the context of John's life. So let's take a closer look at that life.

An Unusual Childhood

St. John was born in Antioch around AD 349. His father was a high-ranking civil servant named Secundus. His mother (whom we met briefly in the last chapter) was Anthousa.

Shortly after the boy's birth, Secundus died, leaving Anthousa a widow at age twenty. She could have remarried, but she chose to follow the biblical counsel "to the unmarried and the widows…to remain single" (1 Corinthians 7:8). It was relatively common in those days for Christian women to enroll themselves in the Church's order of widows, committing themselves to a life of prayer, continence, and service.

Anthousa's piety made a deep impression on young John. She set an example he would recall in his later preaching. John also had an aunt, Sabiniana, who served the church of Antioch as a deaconess. Her contemporaries tell us that Sabiniana "conversed intimately with God."[6]

Needless to say, John grew up in an unusual household. We could say it was almost monastic.

During his school years it seemed that John was destined to be a civil servant like his father. But with graduation his desires took a turn for the contemplative. It was around this time that he was baptized. (There was a tendency among serious Christians in the fourth century to defer baptism until adulthood or even late middle age.) Then he and a friend from school decided to form what was called a "brotherhood"—a household where they could share a common life of voluntary poverty, prayer, and contemplation. The young men had gone far with their plans when John broke the news to his mother.

Anthousa hit the roof. She begged John not to make her a widow all over again. He couldn't resist her pleading, so he agreed to pursue his life of renunciation at home. He adopted the dress of a monk—a coarse, sleeveless garment. He took up Scripture study under a renowned master, and he applied himself in service to the bishop of Antioch.

After three years of living the disciplines at home, John managed to break free and join the solitaries in the wilderness nearby, on Mount Silpios. He lived in a cave by himself. He did not permit himself to lie down, by day or night. He slept hardly at all; and he went without protection from the extremes of heat and cold. For hours each day he read the Scriptures, memorizing entire books. His diet was wretched.

So zealous was John that he continued these austerities even after his health began to decline. But after two years he needed medical care. So he returned, disappointed, to the city.

Letter to a Friend

It was either while John was on the mountain or sometime soon afterward that one of his companions in the ascetical life, Theodore, began having second thoughts. His folks needed him to run the family business, he explained. And there was a young woman beckoning, by the name of Hermione. In time Theodore erased his name from the rolls of the brotherhood and went home.

The situation demanded a response from John, and that response has come down to us with the title *Letter to Theodore After His Fall*. We have it in two parts, totaling twenty-four thousand words. They are the words of a furious man shaking his friend by the lapels.

> Would you have me speak of the domestic cares of wife and children?… It is an evil thing to wed a very poor wife, or a very rich one; for the former is injurious to the husband's means, the latter to his authority and independence. It is a grievous thing to have children, still more grievous not to have any.… Is this then life, Theodore, when one's soul is distracted in so many directions, when a man has to serve so many, to live for so many, and never for himself?[7]

The rhetoric heats up and boils over, as John tries to show the transitory nature of bodily beauty and the grossness of its constituent parts.

> You are now admiring the grace of Hermione, and you judge that there is nothing in the world to be compared to her comeliness; but… the groundwork of this bodily beauty is nothing but phlegm, blood, rheum, bile, and the fluid of digested food.… Consider what is stored inside those beautiful eyes, that straight nose, and the mouth and cheeks, and you will affirm the

well-shaped body to be nothing but a whited sepulchre; the parts within are full of so much uncleanness.[8]

John goes on to compare such illusory and passing beauty with the true and lasting beauty of the soul of a monk steeped in prayer. Needless to say, the earthly beauty comes up the loser.

John is careful to acknowledge that marriage is an honorable estate, citing Hebrews 13:4, but it cannot be honorable for Theodore. "'Marriage is right,' you say; and I agree.… Nevertheless, it is no longer possible for you to observe the right conditions of marriage. For if he who has been attached to a heavenly bridegroom deserts him and joins himself to a wife, the act is…worse than adultery in proportion as God is greater than man."[9]

For these passages John has been vilified by secularists, radical feminists, and hedonists. But his over-the-top statements need to be considered in context—in the context of the immediate situation and in the context of his life's work.

John was, after all, operating in crisis mode. His friend had gone back on a lifelong commitment, checked himself out of the holy brotherhood. Theodore was breaking a promise he had made to God. John recognized this as an emergency demanding forceful intervention; it was a time for tough love.

So he used his rhetoric the way some men might use their muscles. And he succeeded in talking Theodore back into the brotherhood. Theodore would go on to become one of the most influential theologians in antiquity, the celebrated bishop of Mopsuestia.

We should note again that John probably had, at this point, only the remotest experience of normal family life—mom, dad, and kids. I'm not saying that his upbringing was warped or harmful, nor am I sneering at his formation by the hermits. I think both periods gave him the discipline he would need to withstand the hardships of his later life. But they were unusual circumstances, to say the least, and they hardly equipped him for a realistic view of domestic life.

Meeting Christian Families

As John emerged from relative isolation and entered the bustling life of the church of Antioch, he grew to appreciate marriage not as a mere concession to weakness or a second-class citizenship in the Church but as a distinct vocation from God and path to holiness. Even more than that, he came to see it as a powerful *image* of God in the world—a sacrament of God.

But that awakening came only with time and experience.

John's gifts were evident to his bishop. In 381 he was ordained a deacon and licensed to preach. It was then that he earned the nickname *Chrysostom* ("Golden Mouth"), as his sermons drew enormous crowds to church. After five years as a deacon, he was ordained to the priesthood.

The first decade of John's priesthood was a time of intense pastoral work in the second city of the empire. During that time he encountered many families, *real* families, *ordinary* families, *Christian* families. He shared their lives. He counseled them. In a moving expression of his love, he told his congregation: "I know no other life but you and the care of souls."[10]

And what did John learn from all that work with all those souls, through all those years?

The first of the sermons in which we find his mature teaching on marriage are his homilies on First Corinthians. A few years later he would return to the same themes in his homilies on Ephesians and Colossians and his sermons on vainglory. Notice the difference from his earlier teachings:

"There is nothing that so welds our life together as the love of a man and his wife."[11]

"There is nothing in the world sweeter for a man than having children and a wife."[12]

John was not just blowing smoke. He had come to the conclusion that Christian marriage was as much a divine vocation as Syrian monasticism—and that Christian perfection was, by God's grace, attainable in marriage. Our preacher laments to his people: "Why, it is just this that makes me sigh—that you think that *monks* are the only persons properly concerned with decency and chastity."[13]

In the strongest terms he assures his congregation that their calling is nothing less than perfection. He says: "If the beatitudes were spoken only to solitaries, and the secular person cannot fulfill them, yet [Jesus] permitted marriage anyway—then all things have perished, and Christian virtue is boxed in."

But that cannot be the case. And so he continues: "If persons have been hindered by their marriage state, let them know that *marriage* is not the hindrance, but rather *their intentions*, which made an ill use of marriage."[14]

Guidance in the Mysteries

What caused John's apparent change of heart? Had he grown worldly, as pastors sometimes do, concerned as they are with budgets and leaky roofs? Was he bought off by lamb dinners served up by the pious ladies of the parish?

No. For we're told that he continued to live by all the monastic disciplines, including fairly rigorous fasting, and that he always took his meager meals alone.

I believe that John grew in his appreciation for marriage as he grew in the work of Christian initiation—as he taught group after group of new Christians to appreciate the radical transformation that God was working in their lives through the divinizing sacraments. In a city like Antioch in the late fourth century, a pastor could prepare hundreds of adult converts every year. He would lead them to the mysteries, and he would tell them of the mysteries. In baptism God would give them new eyes of faith, and John would teach them to open those eyes.

This is what the Church calls *mystagogy*—the doctrine of the mysteries, guidance in things hidden "since the foundation of the world" (Matthew 13:35). The mystagogue guides the new Christian through the external, material appearances to grasp the unseen reality that is interior, spiritual, hidden, and divine.

When it's used as a technical term in theology, *mystagogy* describes the period of Christian initiation that takes place immediately after the first reception of the sacraments. In the ancient Church this often consisted of daily homilies throughout the Octave of Easter— eight days of sermons that revealed doctrines that had, till then, been kept secret: the doctrine of the real presence of Jesus in the Eucharist, the doctrine of the sanctifying grace of baptism. The preacher would go step by step through the rites, describing the ritual words and gestures and, more importantly, explaining their divine meaning and action.

John would tell his class of new Christians: "What is performed here requires faith and the eyes of the soul: we are not merely to notice what is seen, but to go from this to imagine what cannot be seen. Such is the power of the eyes of faith.… For faith is the capacity to attend to the invisible as if it were visible."[15]

John spoke these words in his baptismal mystagogy. But he hardly confined this approach to his liturgical theology. A mystagogical quality *pervades* John's works. We see it in his homilies on the Letter to the Hebrews. It is everywhere in his treatise on the priesthood. And, I contend, it is the principle that gives life to his mature doctrine of marriage.

We could honestly and accurately describe this teaching as a *mystagogy of marriage*. John wants the people to move from the icon to the reality. Still he insists that they must also learn to venerate the icon. "Learn the power of the type," he says, "so that you may learn the strength of the truth."[16]

It's important for us to realize that John's mature doctrine of marriage is almost unique in ancient Christianity. His contemporaries tended to look upon marriage as an institution that was passing away, as more and more Christians turned to celibacy. In John's day there were 3,000 consecrated virgins and widows in Antioch, a city whose population was perhaps 250,000. *Three thousand celibate women*—and that number doesn't include any of the celibate *men* in brotherhoods or the hermits who inhabited the nearby mountains.

Catholic theologian John Cavadini wryly observes that this was hardly the golden age of the theology of marriage. Many of the Fathers ignore marriage or treat it as a somewhat distasteful subject. The best thing John's contemporary Jerome could say about marriage was that it produced future celibates!

Yet John, in his later years, *glorified* marriage. It pained him that Christian couples continued to practice the old, obscene pagan wedding customs. So shameful were these practices that few couples dared to invite their parish priests to attend and give a blessing. The situation roused our hero to a passionate exhortation: "Is the wedding then a theater? It is a *sacrament*, a *mystery*, and a *model of the Church of Christ*…. They dance at pagan ceremonies; but at ours, silence and decorum should prevail, respect and modesty. Here a great mystery is accomplished."[17]

No Reason to Blush

Marriage is a *sacrament*, a *mystery*, a *model of the Church*. This is the language of mystagogy, and it has deep biblical roots. John grounded his doctrine firmly in St. Paul's Letter to the Ephesians 5:31–32: "'For this reason a man shall leave his father and mother and be joined to his wife, and the two shall become one flesh.' This is a great *mystery*," St. Paul says, "and I mean in reference to Christ and the Church."

St. Paul then has included marriage among the great mysteries of Christianity. But he is digging deep to do so, drawing from the first chapters of Genesis. Indeed, any preacher who memorized most of the Scriptures, as John Chrysostom did, would notice that marriage is a dominant theme in both the Old and New Testaments. The Bible begins with the wedding of Adam and Eve and ends with the marriage supper of the Lamb. And in between these events, God, speaking through the prophets, repeatedly invokes marriage as the preeminent symbol of his covenant (see Hosea 2).

John sees in marriage an image of baptism, where the believer is wed to Christ; and it is an image of the Eucharist, which makes "one flesh" of the believer and Christ. He tells the new Christians: "Keep the marriage robe in its integrity, that with it you may enter forever into this spiritual marriage…. Just as in marriage between man and woman the bridal feast is prolonged for seven days, see how we too extend for the same number of days your bridal feast, setting before you the table of the mysteries, filled with good things beyond number."[18]

Marriage, moreover, is an icon of the Trinity. John teaches, "The child is a bridge connecting mother to father, so the three become one flesh…. And here the bridge is formed from the substance of each!"[19]

At that point John must have looked out at a congregation full of people fanning themselves and averting their eyes, because he was moved to cry out,

> Why are you blushing? Leave that to the heretics and pagans, with their impure and immodest customs. For this reason I want marriage to be thoroughly purified, to bring it back again to its proper nobility. You should not be ashamed of these things. If you are ashamed, then you condemn God who made marriage. So I shall tell you how marriage is a mystery of the Church![20]

John did not want Christians to blush at the mention of married love. But most of all he wanted them to have *no reason to blush*.

Among all the ancient mystagogues, John stands out for his unique emphasis on morals. He insists that the sacraments should leave their mark on everything we do in life. We don't check the mysteries at the door when we leave church on Sunday. The sacraments have consequences for every moment of every day. Through baptism and the Eucharist, we become "partakers of the divine nature" (2 Peter 1:4). John would have us then live our marriages purely, as Christ lives his.

And John speaks plainly. He doesn't care if he makes parishioners squirm. I think it's fair to say that none of the Fathers preached as frankly on sexual matters as he did.

What did this mean practically?

John condemns adultery, domestic violence, sodomy, abortion, divorce, and other acts that are unworthy of the sacrament. And he repeatedly condemns contraception as unworthy of Christian marriage, even calling it preemptive murder:

> Why do you sow where the field is eager to destroy the fruit?
> Where there are medicines of sterility? Where there is murder
> before birth? Indeed, it is something worse than murder and I do
> not know what to call it; for [the woman] does not kill what is
> formed but prevents its formation. What then? Do you despise
> the gift of God, and fight with his law?[21]

John sees birth control as a violation of the type, a desecration of
the icon, a defiling of the sacrament. For if marriage is a sacrament
of God, then it should be a true communion that is fruitful, as
God is.

The Strength of True Marriage

I don't think marriage can get any better than John Chrysostom, in
his mature years, made it out to be. For a married man or woman
to read his homilies on Colossians and Ephesians is to simultane-
ously be exalted and humbled: exalted because God has lifted us up
so high, humbled because we must confront our own sin, our own
clinging to the mud of this earth.

John learned to love marriage, and we should too. As a celibate he
lost nothing in the bargain. For if a celibate renounces something
second-rate, that's not such a big deal. But if he renounces something so great as holy matrimony, a sign of the Trinity, in order to
live with the Trinity *even now* as an angel in heaven—if he
renounces the *sign* in order to possess the *Signified*—then the value
of celibacy increases by orders of magnitude.

As John himself said: "Whoever denigrates marriage also dimin-
ishes the glory of virginity. Whoever praises it makes virginity more
admirable and resplendent. What appears good only in comparison
with evil would not be particularly good. It is something better than
what is admitted to be good that is the most excellent good."[22]

Learn the power of the type, so that you may learn the strength of the truth. We should ponder too the words with which John closed his earthly life: "Glory to God for *all* things! Amen!"[23]

The Case for Celibacy

In our sex-addled world the idea of celibacy seems not only imprac-
tical but impossible. Strangely enough, that's just how it seemed in
the earliest days of the Christian Church.

The Roman Empire was not renowned for its sexual restraint.
We've already been through the ugly excesses of that culture (see
chapter eight)—excesses that strikingly resemble those of our
own time.

The Jews saw fruitful marriage as the ideal state. You were blessed
if you had children; you were cursed if you were "barren." But we
can see some idea of celibacy as an especially holy state in the Old
Testament. Before going up Mount Sinai to speak to God, Moses
told the Israelites, "Be ready by the third day; do not go near a
woman" (Exodus 9:15). The Levites refrained from marital relations
during their regular times of service in the temple (see 1 Samuel
21:3–6; Exodus 19:15; Deuteronomy 23:9–13). And we know that
members of some Jewish sects, such as the Essenes, practiced a form
of celibacy.

For the Sake of the Kingdom
With Christianity celibacy arises as an important theme—and for
good reasons. Jesus lived a celibate life, as did St. John the Baptist
and St. Paul.

As Jesus announced the arrival of the kingdom, he spoke of others who would be celibate for the sake of that kingdom (see Matthew 19:12). He spoke of disciples who would renounce all family ties and receive abundant rewards for doing so (Mark 10:28–30). Even on earth they would live unmarried, "like angels in heaven" (Mark 12:25). But Jesus warned his disciples that not everyone would understand the idea (Matthew 19:11).

Some twenty years later the idea of sexual renunciation was part of the fabric of the Church's life. Paul dedicates much of chapter seven of his First Letter to the Corinthians to the idea. He says that even married couples may decide to live celibate "by agreement for a season, that you may devote yourselves to prayer" (1 Corinthians 7:5).

The general rule, Paul says, is that people will be married: "[E]ach man should have his own wife and each woman her own husband" (1 Corinthians 7:2). That isn't because marriage is better than celibacy, however.

> I say this by way of concession, not of command. I wish that all were as I myself am. But each has his own special gift from God, one of one kind and one of another.
>
> To the unmarried and the widows I say that it is well for them to remain single as I do. But if they cannot exercise self-control, they should marry. For it is better to marry than to be aflame with passion.
>
> To the married I give charge, not I but the Lord, that the wife should not separate from her husband (but if she does, let her remain single or else be reconciled to her husband)—and that the husband should not divorce his wife. (1 Corinthians 7:7–11)

The advice Paul gives is very practical. He knows what people are like, and he recommends the best way to keep them out of trouble. But if you were striving for something better, what would that be?

> Now concerning the unmarried, I have no command of the Lord, but I give my opinion as one who by the Lord's mercy is trustworthy. I think that in view of the impending distress it is well for a person to remain as he is. Are you bound to a wife? Do not seek to be free. Are you free from a wife? Do not seek marriage. But if you marry, you do not sin, and if a girl marries she does not sin. Yet those who marry will have worldly troubles, and I would spare you that. I mean, brethren, the appointed time has grown very short; from now on, let those who have wives live as though they had none, and those who mourn as though they were not mourning, and those who rejoice as though they were not rejoicing, and those who buy as though they had no goods, and those who deal with the world as though they had no dealings with it. For the form of this world is passing away. (1 Corinthians 7:25–31)

It's easy to smirk at Paul here: He thought the world was about to end, and here we are, almost two thousand years later. But think of the times ahead for the early Christians. It would be only a few years before serious persecutions would start—persecutions that would kill both Paul and Peter among countless others. Shortly after that Jerusalem—the center of the Jewish religion and the birthplace of Christianity—would be destroyed. Paul was right: The secure old world as Christians had known it was passing away, and the time of tribulation was about to begin.

When that happened, who would be better off? Christians with families would have their families to worry about; Christians without families could go joyfully to martyrdom if they had to go.

For each of us, in every age, a world is always winding down. The time grows short. That's exactly the reason Paul gives for his advice.

> I want you to be free from anxieties. The unmarried man is anxious about the affairs of the Lord, how to please the Lord; but the married man is anxious about worldly affairs, how to please his wife, and his interests are divided. And the unmarried woman or virgin is anxious about the affairs of the Lord, how to be holy in body and spirit; but the married woman is anxious about worldly affairs, how to please her husband. I say this for your own benefit, not to lay any restraint upon you, but to promote good order and to secure your undivided devotion to the Lord. (1 Corinthians 7:32–35)

A Grassroots Movement

One of the first things we need to remember about celibacy in the early Church is that it wasn't a rule handed down from some administrative official. Modern people often make that mistake when talking about the subject. The truth is that it was a grassroots movement, a groundswell of popular feeling. Thousands of Christians willingly took on the admittedly heavy burden of celibacy because of the much heavier burdens it freed them from.

The first-century letter of St. Clement of Rome and the second-century letters of St. Ignatius of Antioch speak of celibacy and warn those who are celibate to avoid pride and boasting because of the greatness of their life. In the middle of the second century, two apologists—St. Justin Martyr and Athenagoras of Athens—wrote of the "many" Christians, "both men and women," who lived lifelong celibacy.[1]

It's hard to express how different Christianity was from the pagan world when it came to the idea of celibacy. Perhaps the best way to express it is to say that the pagan world saw celibacy in very much the same way our modern secular world sees it: an impossible and unnatural ideal, worthy of sarcasm and snickering. Even the Stoics, whose philosophy was based on detachment from worldly desires, thought celibacy was a nice idea but humanly impossible.

Yet Christians seemed to be falling all over each other in their rush to take on vows of celibacy. Did some of them stumble and break their vows? Of course they did; Christians are sinners, and it was a heavy burden they took on. But many more did not stumble, and their dedication astonished the pagans.

Galen, the personal physician of Marcus Aurelius (who, besides being a capable emperor, was one of the most distinguished philosophers of the Stoic school), had little use for Christian thought. In dismissing stubborn thinkers who accepted everything previous philosophers had taught them, Galen could think of only one thing worse: "You might as well try to teach something new to the followers of Moses and Christ."[2]

Yet even Galen had to admit that the Christians were pretty good at living up to the ideals that philosophers admired:

> So we see that the people who are called "Christians" take their faith from parables, not argument. And yet we sometimes see them acting like philosophers. For every day makes it obvious how much they despise death. And we can plainly see how they control themselves in sex. For they have, not just men, but even women, who refrain from sexual intercourse all their lives; and they also count certain ones who, in self-discipline and self-control, have reached a level not beneath that of real philosophers.[3]

The Gift of the Body

There were important differences between the Christian idea of celibacy and the Stoics' unreachable ideal. The Stoics found the body to be a necessary evil: You had one, you couldn't get along without it, it made demands, and you responded to those demands. If there was a life after death, it would be a final release of the soul from the body.

But to Christians the body was a gift. Certainly that gift had been corrupted by sin, but the body itself was not evil; it was an essential part of the person. Astonishing the pagans, Christians professed belief in a *bodily* resurrection. Some heretical Christians couldn't deal with that idea, but Tertullian argued for the orthodox side, that salvation would not be meaningful without the resurrection of the body.

> Besides, what else is man but flesh? It was certainly the bodily rather than the spiritual element from which the Author of man's nature gave him his name. "And the Lord God made man of the dust of the ground," not of spiritual essence; this afterwards came from the divine breath: "and man became a living soul."
>
> What, then, is man? Made, beyond doubt, of the dust; and God placed him in paradise, because he *formed* him, not breathed him, into being—man was made of flesh, not of spirit.
>
> Since this is true, how can you contend that your "god" is perfectly good, when he fails, not just in a little detail of man's redemption, but in the whole definition of it? If the salvation of the soul alone is a complete grace, a real mercy, then this is the better life right now—the life we enjoy complete and whole. To rise again only partially will be a punishment, not a liberation.[4]

So Christians didn't believe that the body was evil, but they did believe that they could control the body. By the power of God's grace, they could make the flesh subject to the spirit.

In those earliest centuries celibates experimented with different living arrangements. Some lived together in households, as we saw with St. John Chrysostom. And in urban centers wealthy Christian families, when one of their number decided to "take the veil," sometimes converted their homes into "cloisters" for consecrated virgins or consecrated widows.

Others fled to the wilderness to live a solitary life, as St. Anthony of Egypt did in the mid–third century. Anthony's problem was that he soon attracted a multitude who wished to share his way of life. The local Christians described the phenomenon as a "city in the desert"!

In these ancient experiments we can descry the beginnings of the many forms of celibate life we know today: the vowed and cloistered lives of religious orders; the contemplative lives of monks in monasteries; the quiet dedication of consecrated virgins in our dioceses; the celibacy in the midst of the world practiced by members of Opus Dei; and the special path of the secular institutes, in the world and not of the world but for the world.

Celibacy Comes From Heaven

Why were the Christians successful with celibacy, when most of the pagans thought it an impossible ideal?

Ambrose explains that it is because Christ himself, born of a virgin, came into our flesh to make our flesh divine. So the heavenly way of life, in which the blessed "neither marry nor are given in marriage" (Mark 12:25), now becomes possible for earthly mortals. And that heavenly way of life is not a celibacy of abstinence, defined by a negative. It is the greatest of all joys, a marriage to Christ himself.

> But who can understand by mere human power what is not even part of the law of nature? Who can describe in ordinary words

what is beyond nature's scope? Virginity brought down from heaven, what on earth virginity may imitate.

It is fitting that she has looked for her way of life in heaven, when she has found her Spouse in heaven. Passing beyond the clouds, the air, the angels, the stars, she has found the Word of God in the very bosom of the Father, and has wholeheartedly brought him into herself. For who, having found such a great good, would ever leave it? "Your name is oil poured out; therefore the maidens love you; draw me after you" [Song of Solomon 1:3–4].

In fact, what I have said comes not from me, since they who "neither marry nor are given in marriage" are "like angels in heaven" [Mark 12:25]. We should not be surprised if they are compared to angels, when they are united to the Lord of angels.

Then who can deny that it comes from heaven, this way of life that is so hard to find on earth, except after God came down into the members of an earthly body? A Virgin conceived, and "the Word became flesh" [John 1:14] so that flesh might become God....

But after the Lord, coming in our flesh, united divinity and flesh without any confusion or mixture, then the heavenly way of life, spreading through the whole world, was established in human bodies.[5]

Ambrose writes to praise consecrated virginity and deliberately heaps up the attractions of it in his rhetoric. On the other hand, we can turn to crotchety old St. Jerome for a more realistic view.

Celibacy Is Hard Work

Writing to a woman who had taken on what Ambrose described as a blessed, joyous state of marriage to Christ, Jerome warns her that it won't be a walk in the park. One of the remarkable things about Jerome is that many of his correspondents were women, and he always treated them as his intellectual equals. He never watered down his language for delicate female sensibilities: He gave them straight talk, trusting that they could handle it as well as he could.

I'm writing to you, Lady Eustochium—I must call the bride of the Lord "Lady"—to tell you straight off that I'm not going to be praising the virginity you pursue. We can see what it's worth in you anyway. I won't be going over the difficulties of marriage —pregnancy, babies crying, the torture of jealousy, household drudgery, and all those supposed blessings that last until you die. (Not that married women are beyond hope. They have their own place: an honorable marriage and an undefiled bed.)

No, I'm writing to show you that you're running away from Sodom, and you should take a lesson from Lot's wife.

You won't find any flattery in what I write. A flatterer gives you pretty words, but he's still your enemy. Don't expect any fancy rhetoric where I place you among the angels and tell you how your blessed virginity sets the universe at your feet.

No, I don't want you to be proud of your monastic vow. I want you to be afraid. You're carrying gold, so look out for robbers. This life is a race course: we run the race here, but we get our prize somewhere else. You can't set aside fear when there are snakes and scorpions in your path. . . .

Hosts of enemies surround us on every side. The weak flesh will be dust soon enough. It fights against tremendous odds— one against many. Not until it has dissolved—not until the Prince of this world has come and found no sin in it—not until then can you safely listen to the words of the prophet:

> You will not fear the terror of the night,
>
> nor the arrow that flies by day,
>
> nor the pestilence that stalks in darkness,
>
> nor the destruction that wastes at noonday.
>
> A thousand may fall at your side,
>
> ten thousand at your right hand;
>
> but it will not come near you. (Psalm 91:5–7)[6]

We can see what people were commonly saying about consecrated virginity just from what Jerome tells her he won't be saying: You're already an angel. You have the world at your feet. Balderdash, says Jerome. Celibacy is a grace, but responding to that grace requires effort. Celibacy, like anything else that's worthwhile, is hard work.

Still, just from the fact that Jerome has to acknowledge those notions, we know that there was already a high regard for consecrated virginity in Christian culture. It was an attractive state, something to be admired and something to be aspired to.

Missing Grace

Jerome made many enemies with his blunt speaking, and he was never blunter than when he found people who had taken on vows of poverty and celibacy but didn't live up to them. Sulpitius Severus recounts a conversation he and a monk from Gaul had with his friend Postumanius, who had just returned from the East, and, in particular, the reaction Postumanius got from their Gaulish friend when, in the course of narrating his travels, he brought up the name of Jerome.

> "So [Postumanius continued] I set out and headed for Bethlehem, which is six miles outside Jerusalem, but takes sixteen days if you go from Alexandria. The priest Jerome is in

charge of the church here, since it is a parish of the bishop of Jerusalem.

"I had already got to know Jerome in my previous journey, and that acquaintance was enough to persuade me that no one was more worthy of my respect and love. Aside from the esteem he earns by his faith and his many virtues, he is learned not only in Latin and Greek, but in Hebrew as well, so that no one dares compare himself to Jerome in all knowledge. I'd be very surprised if you don't know him very well through the books he has written, since it seems the whole world reads him."

"Actually," the Gaul said, "we know him only too well. About five years ago, I read a book of his in which he fiercely attacks and reviles our whole tribe of monks. Our Belgian friend is still angry at him because he says we stuff our faces all the time. As for me, I forgive the eminent man. After all, a love of eating may be gluttony to the Greeks, but with us Gauls it's just our nature."

"That's a good rhetorical defense of your nation," I said. "But I must ask, is that the only monkish vice his book condemns?"

"Certainly not," he replied. "The writer didn't leave anything out. He chastised, scourged, and exposed everything. In particular, he railed against greed and arrogance. He had a lot to say about pride, and a good bit about superstition. And I have to say I thought he painted a pretty accurate picture of the vices of a lot of people.

"But when it came to the familiarities between virgins and monks, how true—and how brave—his words were! And because of what he said there, I hear he is not very much in favor with certain people, not mentioning any names. Just like our Belgian friend, who got angry because he said we like eating too much, those people (I hear) are furious when they read in that little book, 'The virgin despises her true unmarried brother, and looks for a stranger.'"[7]

Jerome's invective tells us a lot about the state of monasticism in his time. It was no longer a matter of a few dedicated Christians separating themselves from society: it had become a large-scale movement, and it was attracting a lot of people who weren't really suited to the life. It was not a question of the Church trying to lure people into the monasteries; on the contrary, the Church couldn't keep them away!

CHAPTER ELEVEN

Defending Human Life: The Early Church and Abortion

There's been a bit of debate lately on what the early Church thought of abortion. That's surprising when you think about it, because we'd give a lot to have the kind of documentary record for other doctrines that we have for the Church's condemnation of this practice.

The issue arises in the earliest texts: the *Didache* and *Epistle of Barnabas* in the first century; the apologies of Athenagoras and Justin in the second; the theology of Origen and Hippolytus in the third; and the decrees of the early councils in the fourth. And that's just a small sampling. No other moral issue has such a detailed paper trail. Even the earliest documents—most of them very brief—take time to state an unqualified condemnation of the practice.

The Fathers spoke with such certainty, clarity, and consistency on the issue that it's hard to find any seams in the argument. That's all the more remarkable when we consider how the popular culture of the time treated children, as we already discussed in chapter nine.

Abortion Is Murder

Pagan philosophers would have been inclined to agree with today's abortion protesters: Abortion is baby-killing. The difference is that the pagan philosophers didn't see anything wrong with killing babies. Infanticide was a common and well-accepted practice in the pagan world. Romans didn't always kill their babies directly; more often they "exposed" them, meaning that they threw them out on the trash heap to die of starvation and exposure. Girl babies, of course, were especially disposable. Many a Christian woman grew from one of those exposed babies whom some passing Christian discovered and rescued.

Abortion was a well-known practice in classical medicine. We know this from the ancient medical textbooks that have survived. Tertullian discusses it in many of his works, and always as the equivalent of infanticide. In one place he gives a careful description of the medical instruments involved:

> The surgeons have a certain instrument among their tools. For opening the uterus, first of all, it has a delicately adjusted flexible frame. While it holds the uterus open, it has a ring-shaped blade, with which the surgeon very carefully cuts up the limbs inside the womb. Finally, it has a blunt or coated hook to extract the whole fetus with a violent delivery. The surgeons also have a copper needle or spike, by which the actual death is managed in this stealthy murder. Because it's made for infanticide, they call *itembryosphactes,* the baby-killer—because the baby was of course alive. These instruments were in the possession of Hippocrates, Asclepiades, Erasistratus, Herophilus (who even dissected adults), and mild-mannered Soranus himself. They all knew very well that a living being had been conceived, and pitied this terribly unfortunate infant.[1]

Tertullian wasn't approving of abortion: He was merely describing it as part of his argument that the infant already had a soul inside the womb. Many pagans held that the soul entered only at birth, but

Tertullian observed that all the most eminent doctors knew otherwise. The child was alive. That's why they called their instruments "baby-killers."

Athenagoras wrote to defend the Christians to the philosopher-emperor Marcus Aurelius in about the year 177. One of the constant charges against the Christians—obviously based on a bizarre misunderstanding of the Eucharist—was that they killed and ate people. Athenagoras gives many reasons why this can't be so, among them the fact that Christians even regard abortion as murder, so how could they murder someone already born?

> So if this is what Christians are like, what sane man will call us murderers? After all, we can't eat human flesh unless we've killed someone.... But when people know that we can't even bear to see a man put to death, who can accuse us of murder or cannibalism?
>
> Now, everyone thinks it's a great spectacle to see the games with gladiators and wild animals (especially the ones you give!). But we think that even seeing a man put to death is a lot like killing him, so we won't go to the games.
>
> Then how could we put people to death, when we won't even look at the games for fear of guilt and pollution?
>
> We say that women who use drugs to bring on an abortion are committing murder, and they will have to give an account to God. So how could we commit murder? The same person can't insist that the very fetus in the womb is a created being cared for by God, and then kill it after it's born. The same person can't condemn exposing infants as murdering children, and then destroy the child after it's grown up. No, we're always consistent in everything. We submit to reason; we don't bend reason to our will.[2]

The second-century *Letter to Diognetus* (by an author whose name is lost to us) draws a strong contrast between Christians and the world around them: Among many other things, "they marry, as everyone else does; they have children; but they do not destroy their offspring." Because of these differences the Christians "live in their own countries, but only as foreigners."[3] If you didn't destroy your children, you were hardly recognizable as a Roman!

We can see what early Christians thought of abortion just as clearly in the writings of St. Hippolytus of Rome, who wrote his *Refutation of All Heresies* around the year 200. Describing the alleged heresy of Callistus, he goes into shocking detail:

> He even allowed unmarried girls, if they were burning with passion (at an age that would be inappropriate anyway), or if they didn't want to compromise their position with a legal marriage, to go to bed with whoever appealed to them, slave or free. Even if they weren't legally married, he said, a woman could consider a bedfellow like that her husband.
>
> So women who called themselves believers started to use drugs to sterilize themselves. They would wrap bindings around themselves to squeeze out the fetus they conceived, because they didn't want to have a child by a slave or any old lowlife—they preferred their noble families and their extravagant riches.
>
> Do you see how far that outlaw has fallen into impiety? He teaches adultery and murder at the same time! Yet even after such outrages, they still shamelessly call themselves a "Catholic" Church![4]

For orthodox Christianity abortion is the willful taking of an innocent life. Hippolytus called it murder: You couldn't make the equivalence clearer than that.

Three Sins in One

The Christian stance on abortion clearly set the early Church apart from a culture that said there was no problem with abortion and that even condoned infanticide. It is a situation familiar to twenty-first-century Catholics: the Church had to stand up against a popular culture that told women, "Here's how you solve your little problem." Through the ages the Church has had to make its position explicit over and over again.

It's worth knowing that standing against abortion didn't set the early Christians apart from Jews, who were just as much against it. But Christians had to deal with the problem more because they enthusiastically evangelized pagans. Their new converts had to be taught that there were some cultural norms that just couldn't be brought into the Church.

Separating from the culture of death has continued to be an issue for the Church. By the time of St. Jerome, Christianity had been the official religion of the Roman Empire for some time, and it was quite fashionable for women of good breeding to enter religious communities. Though Christian in name, some still needed to learn to act like Christians.

> I can't even bear to mention the many virgins who fall every day and are lost to the bosom of their mother the Church—stars above which the proud Enemy has set his throne (Isaiah 14:13), and rocks hollowed out by the Serpent so that he can live in the cracks.
>
> You'll find many women who are widows before they're married. They try to hide their shame with lying clothes. Unless a bulging stomach or a crying baby betrays them, they walk in the open with confident steps and heads held high. Some even go so

far as to take some concoction to make themselves barren, murdering human beings almost before they're conceived. Some, when they find themselves pregnant through their sin, use drugs for an abortion. And when—as it often happens—they die along with their children, they go down to the world beneath bearing the guilt, not only of adultery against Christ, but also of suicide and infanticide.[5]

For Jerome abortion isn't just one horrible sin: It's a three-part complex of sin. First there's the adultery or fornication that makes abortion a temptation. Then there's suicide—because often the attempts at abortion were fatal to the mother as well. (That still happens more often than we'd like to think.) Finally, of course, there's the murder of the innocent child.

St. Augustine and the Quickening Question

But what about St. Augustine? Didn't he say that abortion was all right up to a certain point?

If we watch the nightly news, we will sometimes hear pro-abortion politicians make this rather incredible claim. They base that claim, of course, on outright abuse of one of Augustine's texts.

It's a bit ironic to see Augustine pressed into service for the pro-choice agenda. His argument depends on his outdated ideas of embryology, not to mention his fifth-century notions of the inferiority of females. According to Augustine's best information, the male fetus became a person, or was "vivified," at thirty days from conception, whereas the obviously inferior female fetus became a person at ninety days.

Do we really want to rely on those ideas? We know now that a fetus is wonderfully differentiated at three months—and makes a pretty picture on an ultrasound monitor—and its development does not depend upon maleness or femaleness.

And of course Augustine wasn't arguing for abortion license. He wasn't saying that abortion is quite all right until a fetus is "vivified." No, he was trying to decide whether abortion should be classified as a simple mortal sin or the civil crime of murder. Those were the only choices.

Augustine was a careful thinker, as we can see from how deeply he went into the question of the eternal destination of a miscarried fetus:

> This question, therefore, may be very carefully looked into and discussed by the learned, though I do not know whether it is in man's power to resolve it: When does the infant begin to live in the womb? Does life exist in a latent form before it manifests itself in the motions of the living being?
>
> It seems too much to say that the young who, having died in the womb, are cut out limb by limb to save the mother's life, have never been alive. Now, as soon as a man begins to live, it is possible for him to die. And if he does die, no matter where death comes for him, I can find no reason for denying him a part in the resurrection of the dead.[6]

It may not even be possible to know when life begins, Augustine says. (And indeed it wasn't possible to know *scientifically* in Augustine's time.) He's not willing to make a scientific determination based on the knowledge he has, and he doubts whether anyone else can do it. But the Christian can safely assume that, even if a living child dies in the womb, that child has a part in the resurrection.

When it came to the morality of abortion, however, Augustine saw no reason to tread carefully. He condemns contraception in no uncertain terms. It leads to infanticide, and he can scarcely believe that some even go beyond that to abortion:

ROOTS OF THE FAITH

Those who resort to contraception, though we call them spouses, are really no such things. They have no scrap of true marriage left, but pretend to be married as a screen for their criminal activities.

Once they've gone that far, they're seduced into exposing the children born against their will. They hate to keep and raise the children they were afraid to conceive in the first place.

Inflicting such cruelty on children they were so reluctant to conceive unmasks the sin they had done in the dark, and drags it into the clear daylight. The open cruelty condemns the hidden sin.

Sometimes, in fact, this lustful cruelty, or—if you'd rather—this cruel lust, resorts to such outrageous methods as using poisons to make the woman sterile. Or, if that doesn't work, the couple will destroy the fetus somehow before it's born. They'd rather their offspring perish before it lives—or if it has begun to live, that it should be killed before it's born.

Well, if the couple are both so disgracefully perverted, they are not husband and wife. If they started out so perverted, then they came together not by marriage but by debauchery. But if the two are not both such sinners, then I tell you plainly, either the woman is (so to speak) the husband's whore, or the man is the wife's adulterer.[7]

Augustine doesn't know whether the fetus is vivified yet, and his scientific mind won't let him ignore that possible distinction. But he doesn't have to know that to know that abortion is extravagantly evil. It doesn't look as though anyone should put St. Augustine on the "pro-choice" side.

So what we see when we look at the paper trail—St. Augustine included—is a uniform, unvarying record of standing up for life. It takes courage to stand up for life today, when the culture wants us to ignore the rights of the unborn child. But it took even more courage in the early days, when the culture didn't believe children had a right to live even after they were born.

Nevertheless, the Church did stand up for life. It was countercultural then, and it's countercultural now. The truth is that the unborn child is a living person. No matter how inconvenient it might be, the Church has never wavered on this stand.

The Return of the Early Christians

So here we are back in the twenty-first century, with our big churches with parking lots and climate control and amplified sound systems. It's a very different world from the world of the early Christians we were just touring.

But our tour has also shown us that things are very much the same as they were back then. The Church grows, but it's the same Church. The world gives us new challenges, but most of them are just variations on the same old challenges.

In the Middle Ages, when the Church was at the peak of its temporal power, many people were Christians because they weren't allowed to be anything else. That doesn't mean there were no sincere, committed believers—on the contrary, there were many great saints. But being a Catholic was the path of least resistance.

Now nobody makes you a Catholic. You can leave the Church whenever you like, and there's hardly a country in the world where you'll suffer any serious penalties for it. If you're a Catholic it's because you want to be.

But people still come to the Church. You can't keep them away. Much of the Church's growth is in places where it really costs something to be Christian—where Christians are actively persecuted. In many parts of the world, a Catholic can be arrested, beaten up, driven from his home, or murdered just for being Christian.

American Catholics like to think they're persecuted in today's secular society, but we don't know anything about real persecution. We do live in a paganized world that puts pleasure at the top of its priority list—a world that seems to be losing its hope for the future. Like the early Christians, we have no power to coerce people to come to the faith. All we have is our example, the Good News, and the grace of God. And that's more than enough.

We're living in an exciting age like that of the early Christians. The secret dream of every enthusiastic Christian—to live in the golden age of the Church—is coming true for us. We're living in a time when the Word can spread only by virtue of its own truth and by divine guidance. And the Word *is* spreading.

Look around you. You're living in an age of great saints. Some of them are people who make an impression in the world, but many of them pass by unnoticed. They're just ordinary people who live their lives the way Christ taught us to live, not because they're made to but because they want to, and by their example they bring more believers to the Church.

Today we can see in the Catholic Church the Church the apostles knew—the Church for which the martyrs died. We know that our tradition goes all the way back to Christ himself. We know that nothing essential has changed. In fact, if we hopped into a time machine and flew back to the days of the martyrs, we'd feel right at home, no matter how different the world around us was.

But Tradition isn't just the past. It's what we pass on to the future as well. We are the witnesses future generations will turn to. They'll look back at us and recognize their own Church, however it may have grown since our time. We're living the history of the Church right now, and it's every bit as exciting as it was in the days of St. Clement and St. Jerome.

The Church will continue, guided by the Holy Spirit. If we stick with the Church, we'll become part of that great cloud of witnesses who testify to the truth. And the truth will set us free, with many of our neighbors, our coworkers, and our friends.

Quotes from the Fathers are adapted from the great collections produced in the nineteenth century: *The Ante-Nicene Fathers* (*ANF*), Alexander Roberts, ed. (Buffalo, N.Y.: Christian Literature, 1885–1896), *The Nicene and Post-Nicene Fathers* (two series, which I've abbreviated *NPNF1* and *NPNF2*), Alexander Roberts, James Donaldson, Philip Schaff, and Henry Wace, eds. (Buffalo, N.Y.: Christian Literature, 1886–1900), and *The Apostolic Fathers* (*TAF*), single-volume edition, J.B. Lightfoot, trans. (London: Macmillan, 1891).

In footnotes I include the series abbreviation and the volume number and page number of the passage referenced. Thus *NPNF2* 1:1 denotes *The Nicene and Post-Nicene Fathers*, Second Series, volume 1, page 1. All the translations are accessible online at newadvent.org, tertullian.org, ccel.org, and elsewhere.

Introduction: Witnesses to Tradition
1. See Joseph Ratzinger's discussion in *Principles of Catholic Theology: Building Stones for a Fundamental Theology* (San Francisco: Ignatius, 1987), pp. 133–152. Ratzinger's work is summarized well in Aidan Nichols, *The Shape of Catholic Theology: An Introduction to Its Sources, Principles, and History* (Collegeville, Minn.: Liturgical, 1991), pp. 205–206.

Chapter One: The Mass: The Universal Sign
1. Ignatius of Antioch, *To the Smyrnaeans* 6–7, adapted from *ANF* 1:88–89.
2. Pliny the Younger, *Letter to Trajan*, adapted from *Internet Ancient Christian Sourcebook*, fordham.edu.
3. Irenaeus of Lyons, *Against the Heresies*, 4.17.5, adapted from *ANF* 1:484.
4. Hippolytus of Rome, *The Apostolic Tradition* 4, Kevin Edgecomb, trans. bombaxo.com.
5. Cyprian, Treatise 4.31, adapted from *ANF* 5:455.
6. Justin Martyr, *Dialogue with Trypho* 41, adapted from *ANF* 1:215.

Chapter Two: Confession: The History of Mercy

1. *Didache*, 14.

2. Aphrahat, *On Penitents* 2–3 (*Demonstrations* 7), adapted from the translation of Frank H. Hallock, *Journal of the Society of Oriental Research* 16 (1932), pp. 43–56, available online at tertullian.org.

3. Hermas, *Commandment* 4.3, adapted from *ANF* 2:22.

4. Tertullian, *On Repentance* 7, adapted from *ANF* 3:663.

5. I have written other books about the Fathers, and with every one of them, some reader has asked why I've quoted from certain ancient writers—specifically Tertullian, Origen, and Eusebius. All three men strayed in matters of doctrine or discipline. My answer is simple: I cite them as authorities because the Catholic Church does.

   In the generation after Tertullian's death, St. Cyprian, the great martyr-bishop of Carthage, referred to him as "The Master" and used his works for spiritual reading. Origen was similarly revered by the great Cappadocian Fathers. Eusebius's history provides the baseline for any study of the development of doctrine. Fairly regularly, and in magisterial documents, the Church invokes the authority of these men. Tradition treats them cautiously but also calls upon them as important witnesses. I feel confident in doing so in this book.

6. Isaiah 3:12 in the Latin version used by St. Cyprian. The English *RSV* translates this verse, "O my people, your leaders mislead you, and confuse the course of your paths."

7. Cyprian of Carthage, *Epistle* 27.2–3, adapted from *ANF* 5:306.

8. Ambrose, *On the Death of Theodosius* 34, *Patrologia Latina* 13:1396.

9. Theodoret, *Ecclesiastical History* 5.17, adapted from *NPNF2* 3:145.

Chapter Three: From the Scriptures to the Bible

1. Justin Martyr, *First Apology* 67, adapted from *ANF* 1:186.

2. Clement of Rome, *To the Corinthians* 45.2–3, adapted from *TAF*, p. 76.

3. Justin Martyr, *Dialogue with Trypho* 68, adapted from *ANF* 1:232.

4. Justin Martyr, *Dialogue with Trypho* 68, adapted from *ANF* 1:232–233.

5. Justin Martyr, *Dialogue with Trypho* 68.

6. Irenaeus of Lyons, *Against the Heresies,* 3.11.8, adapted from *ANF* 1:428.

7. Eusebius of Caesarea, *Church History,* 6.14.1–3, adapted from *NPNF2* 1:261.

8. Polycarp of Smyrna, *To the Philippians* 7, adapted from *ANF* 1:34.
9. Irenaeus of Lyons, *Against the Heresies* 3.3.4, adapted from *ANF* 1:416; see also Eusebius of Caesarea, *Church History* 4.14.
10. Tertullian, *Against Marcion* 1.19, adapted from *ANF* 3:285.
11. Tertullian, *Against Marcion* 1.21, adapted from *ANF* 3:286.
12. Origen, *On First Principles,* Preface, adapted from *ANF* 4:239.
13. Tertullian, *Against Marcion* 4.5 21, adapted from *ANF* 3:349–350.
14. Irenaeus, *Against the Heresies* 3.21.2, adapted from *ANF* 1:451–452.
15. Jerome, *Preface to Job* 21, adapted from *NPNF2* 6:491–492.
16. *Talmud Bavli Qiddushin* 49a.

Chapter Four: The Saints in Heaven: Stones Cry Out
1. *Roman Missal*, Preface for Mass of Christian Death I.
2. Paulinus of Nola, Letter 32.17, in P.G. Walsh, trans., *Letters of St. Paulinus of Nola*, vol. 36, *Ancient Christian Writers* (New York: Newman, 1967), pp. 151–152.
3. Jerome, *Against Vigilantius* 6, adapted from *NPNF2* 6:419.
4. Julian the Apostate, *Against the Galileans* 1, adapted from the translation of W.C. Wright, tertullian.org.
5. Quoted in Adrian Murdoch, *The Last Pagan: Julian the Apostate and the Death of the Ancient World* (Rochester, Vt.: Inner Traditions, 2008), p. 8.
6. Libanius, *Funeral Oration on the Emperor Julian*, adapted from the translation of W.C. Wright, tertullian.org.
7. E. Jeffreys et al., eds., *The Chronicle of John Malalas* (Melbourne: University of Sydney, 1986), pp. 181–182, quoted at www.ucc.ie.

Chapter Five: Purgatory: Love Stronger Than Death
1. Tertullian, *De Corona* 2–3, adapted from *ANF* 3:94.
2. Origen, *Homilies on Jeremiah* 16.5–6, new translation, from *Patrologia Graeca* 13:445, 448.
3. Gregory of Nyssa, *On the Soul and Its Resurrection*, adapted from *NPNF2* 5:451.
4. *Petrvs roga pro sanctis hominibvs Chrestianis ad corpvs tvvm sepvltis.* See Margherita Guarducci, *The Tomb of St. Peter: The New Discoveries in the Sacred Grottoes of the Vatican*, Joseph McLellan, trans. (London: George G. Harrap, 1959), p.146.
5. Augustine of Hippo, *Confessions*, bk. 9, chap. 11.

Chapter Six: The Clergy: Love's Earthly Form

1. Clement of Rome, *To the Corinthians* 42:1–4; 44:1–2, adapted from *TAF*, pp. 75–76.
2. Clement of Rome, *To the Corinthians* 40:3, 5; 41:1, adapted from *TAF*, p. 74.
3. Ignatius of Antioch, *To the Philadelphians* 4, adapted from *ANF* 1:81.
4. Ignatius of Antioch, *To the Magnesians* 6, adapted from *ANF* 1:61.
5. Clement of Alexandria, *Stromata* 6.13, adapted from *ANF* 2:505.
6. Cyprian of Carthage, *Letter* 68.8, adapted from *ANF* 5:374–375.
7. Augustine of Hippo, *Contra epistulam Parmeniani* 2.13, new translation; original online at augustinus.it.
8. John Chrysostom, *On the Priesthood* 3.4, adapted from *NPNF1* 9:46.
9. Ambrose of Milan, *On the Duties of the Clergy* 1.256–258, adapted from *NPNF2* 10:41.
10. Ambrose of Milan, *On the Duties of the Clergy* 2.119–123, adapted from *NPNF2* 10:61–62.
11. Ambrose of Milan, *Against Auxentius* 36 (this paragraph is omitted, without explanation, from the Anglican-edited *NPNF*).
12. Ambrose of Milan, *Against Auxentius* 1, adapted from *NPNF2* 10:430.

Chapter Seven: The Papacy: The Apostolic Throne

1. Clement of Rome, *To the Corinthians* 1, adapted from *TAF*, p. 57.
2. Clement of Rome, *To the Corinthians* 57, 59, adapted from *TAF*, pp. 81–82.
3. Clement of Rome, *To the Corinthians* 63.2, adapted from *TAF*, p. 84.
4. Clement of Rome, *To the Corinthians* 59.1, adapted from *TAF*, p. 82.
5. Ignatius of Antioch, *To the Romans*, preamble, adapted from *ANF* 1:73.
6. Ignatius of Antioch, *To the Magnesians*, preamble, adapted from *ANF* 1:59.
7. Irenaeus of Lyons, *Against the Heresies* 3.3.2, adapted from *ANF* 1:415–416.
8. Irenaeus of Lyons, *Against the Heresies* 3.3.2.
9. Eusebius of Caesarea, *Church History* 7.30.18–19, adapted from *NPNF2* 1:316.
10. Augustine of Hippo, *Sermon* 131.10; Latin text online at augustinus.it.

11. Athanasius, *History of the Arians* 35.2, adapted from *NPNF2* 4:282.

12. Athanasius, *History of the Arians* 36, adapted from *NPNF2* 4:282.

Chapter Eight: Sex and the Sexes

1. F.R. Cowell makes this point in *Life in Ancient Rome* (New York: Putnam, 1961), p. 58. He singles out Catullus for his use of the word *invisa* ("hated" or "detested") to describe daughters.

2. Paul Veyne, *A History of Private Life: From Pagan Rome to Byzantium* (Cambridge, Mass.: Harvard University Press, 1987), p. 34.

3. Clement of Alexandria, *Miscellanies* 2.23.

4. Clement of Alexandria, *Fragment of a Treatise on Marriage*, adapted from *ANF* 2:581.

5. John Chrysostom, *Letter to a Young Widow* 2, adapted from *NPNF1* 9:122.

6. Clement of Alexandria, *Miscellanies* 2.23.

7. Petronius, *Satyricon*, part 2, adapted from e-text at gutenberg.org.

8. Dio Cassius, *Roman History* 63:6, penelope.uchicago.edu.

9. Cyprian, *Of the Discipline and Advantage of Chastity* 11, adapted from *ANF* 5:11.

Chapter Nine: The Mysteries of Marriage

1. Chapter nine is based on a talk given by the author and posted at www.fathersofthechurch.com. An adapted version appeared in *Touchstone Magazine*, January/February 2008.

2. Tertullian, *To His Wife* 2.8.6–7, adapted from *ANF* 4:48.

3. John Chrysostom, as quoted in Uta Ranke-Heinemann, *Eunuchs for the Kingdom of Heaven: Women, Sexuality and the Catholic Church* (New York: Penguin, 1991), p. 236.

4. Peter Brown, *The Body and Society: Men, Women, and Sexual Renunciation in Early Christianity* (New York: Columbia University Press, 1988), pp. 308–309.

5. John Chrysostom, *On Colossians* 12.5, adapted from *NPNF1* 13:319.

6. Palladius, *Dialogue* 5, tertullian.org.

7. John Chrysostom, *Letters to Theodore* 2.5, adapted from *NPNF1* 9:115.

8. John Chrysostom, *Letters to Theodore* 1.14, adapted from *NPNF1* 9:103–104.

9. John Chrysostom, *Letters to Theodore* 2.5, adapted from *NPNF1* 9:113.

10. John Chrysostom, *On the Statues* 9.1, adapted from *NPNF1* 9:399.

11. John Chrysostom, *On Ephesians* 20.1, adapted from *NPNF1* 13:143.

12. John Chrysostom, *On Matthew* 37.9, adapted from *NPNF1* 10:250.

13. John Chrysostom, *On Matthew* 7.8, adapted from *NPNF1* 10:49.

14. John Chrysostom, *On Hebrews* 7.11, adapted from *NPNF1* 14:402.

15. John Chrysostom, *Baptismal Homilies* 2.9, in Edward Yarnold, *The Awe-Inspiring Rites of Initiation: The Origins of the RCIA* (Collegeville, Minn.: Liturgical, 1994), p. 155; see also *Baptismal Instruction* 11.11, vol. 31, *Ancient Christian Writers* (Westminster, Md.: Newman, 1963), p. 164.

16. John Chrysostom, *Baptismal Instruction,* p. 60.

17. John Chrysostom, *On Colossians* 12.5, adapted from *NPNF1* 13:318, compared to the Greek original.

18. John Chrysostom, *Baptismal Instruction,* pp. 103–104.

19. John Chrysostom, *On Colossians* 12.5, adapted from *NPNF1* 13:319.

20. John Chrysostom, *On Colossians* 12.5.

21. John Chrysostom, *On Romans* 24, adapted from *NPNF1* 11:520; see also *On Matthew* 28.5; *On Galatians* 5.12; *On Ephesians* 5.

22. John Chrysostom, *On Virginity* 10, quoted in Pope John Paul II, Apostolic Exhortation *Familiaris Consortio* (1981), no. 16.

23. See Paul Thigpen, *Last Words: Final Thoughts of Catholic Saints & Sinners* (Cincinnati: Servant, 2006), p. 75.

Chapter Ten: The Case for Celibacy

1. Justin Martyr, *First Apology* 29; Athenagoras, *Apology* 33.

2. See Galen, *De Pulsuum Differentiis*, 3.3.

3. Galen made this remark in his commentary on Plato's *Republic.* The work survives only in a few Arabic fragments.

4. Tertullian, *Against Marcion* 1.24, adapted from *ANF* 3:290.

5. Ambrose of Milan, *On Virgins* 1.3, adapted from *NPNF2* 10:365.

6. Jerome, *Letter* 22, 2–3, adapted from *NPNF2* 6:23.

7. Sulpitius Severus, *Dialogue* 1.8–9, adapted from *NPNF2* 11:27–28.

Chapter Eleven: Defending Human Life: The Early Church and Abortion
1. Tertullian, *On the Soul* 25, adapted from *ANF* 3:205–206.
2. Athenagoras, *Plea for the Christians* 35, adapted from *ANF* 2:147.
3. *Epistle to Diognetus* 5, adapted from *ANF* 1:26.
4. Hippolytus of Rome, *Refutation of All Heresies* 9.7, adapted from *ANF* 5:131.
5. Jerome, *Letter* 22.13, adapted from *NPNF2* 6:27.
6. Augustine of Hippo, *Enchiridion* 85, adapted from *NPNF1* 3:265.
7. Augustine of Hippo, *On Marriage and Concupiscence* 1.17, adapted from *NPNF1* 5:271.

ABOUT THE AUTHOR

MIKE AQUILINA is executive vice president of the St. Paul Center for Biblical Theology. He is the author of many books on Church history, doctrine, and devotion, and has hosted several series on EWTN. He is past editor of *New Covenant* magazine. Mike's books include *Angels of God: The Bible, the Church and the Heavenly Hosts, Love in the Little Things, Fire of God's Love: 120 Reflections on the Eucharist,* and *The Fathers of the Church.*